ROBERTA CARDEW

from **Spain** *with love*

11 Quilts Celebrate Mediterranean Color

C&T PUBLISHING

Text copyright © 2010 by Roberta Cardew

Artwork copyright © 2010 by C&T Publishing, Inc.

Quilt and on-location Spanish photography copyright © 2010 by Molly Ware

Publisher: Amy Marson

Creative Director: Gailen Runge

Acquisitions Editor: Susanne Woods

Editor: Cynthia Bix

Technical Editors: Carolyn Aune and Gailen Runge

Copyeditor/Proofreader: Wordfirm Inc.

Cover: Kerry Graham

Book Designer: Rose Sheifer-Wright

Production Coordinators: Jenny Leicester and Kirstie L. Pettersen

Production Editor: Julia Cianci

Illustrator: Aliza Shalit

Photography by Molly Ware

Published by C&T Publishing, Inc., P.O. Box 1456, Lafayette, CA 94549

Library of Congress Cataloging-in-Publication Data

Cardew, Roberta.

From Spain with love : 11 quilts celebrate Mediterranean color / Roberta Cardew.

   p. cm.

ISBN 978-1-57120-937-5 (soft cover)

1. Patchwork--Patterns. 2. Machine quilting--Patterns. I. Title.

TT835.C37154 2010

746.46'041--dc22

                           2009048600

Printed in China

10 9 8 7 6 5 4 3 2 1

Dedication

This book is dedicated to my son Branko without whose encouragement and support I would never have gone to Spain in the first place, and to my father who, for starters, planted a willow tree the day I was born.

Acknowledgments

Heartfelt thanks to so many special people associated with the writing of this book.

First and always, to my family:

My daughter Molly who has taken these wonderful pictures and who is forever ready to put aside personal pursuits in the interests of one of "Mom's projects," for driving me back and forth across coastal Spain, hanging from cliffs, wading through fields, and whatever was necessary for just the right photo shot.

Tonja, my older daughter, who sees to details so that I am free to sew and write, and who tirelessly listens as I run ideas and their endless variations past her night after night when probably she'd rather be home, and for her sincere interest, input, and her valued friendship.

Kim, sister extraordinaire, whose devotion I cherish, for keeping the shop beautiful and operating during my often and sometimes lengthy absences, and for helping me with everything else when I'm present.

And Seth, my very talented husband and friend, who shares with me his ideas about color, proportion, visual rhyme, and banding, and for the very colorful and unique way in which he looks at life and light.

To our wonderful family of customers, who have lent interest, support, encouragement, and valuable comments during the long process of constructing these quilts.

And finally, to C&T Publishing and their great team—especially Cynthia Bix who first suggested I write about color—who have guided me through the book process and, from the onset, were willing to take a chance on a new author and a new idea.

CONTENTS

Introduction

My road to Spain was not a straight one, certainly not as the crow flies. Perhaps this is a strange way to begin a book of patchwork quilt patterns. But to get us to Spain, where the inspiration for the quilts in the book began, we have to start in England— you know, sort of setting the scene.

The Journey

My husband, Seth—an English potter and sculptor whom you will encounter while reading this book—has been a link to a creative world, not just to artists and craftspeople, but to ideas and philosophies. The eldest of three sons of the noted potter Michael Cardew, he inherited the family home in Cornwall and Wenford Bridge Pottery. It was during the Wenford years that I entered the scene.

Wenford Bridge Pottery, originally a proper English coaching inn, was complete with stables, cobbled courtyard, blacksmith shop, and lots and lots of bedrooms. We had guests enough to fill them. Ceramics enthusiasts and devotees—formal students and craftspeople as well as authors, researchers, historians, and even a cultural envoy from Tokyo sent to take photographs—came from all over the world to "worship" at the altar of Michael Cardew's wood-fired kiln and commemorate his life. I was eventually overwhelmed with the mountains of laundry and nonstop cooking of dishes needed to gratify artistic appetites. It was all fantastic, interesting, stimulating, and utterly exhausting.

It was during a low, woe-is-me moment, thinking I just had to escape the crowds, that I remembered a letter we had received several months before from a friend telling us of a house for sale in Spain…perhaps we would be interested…? Preposterous, I had thought at the time—what would we possibly do with a house in Spain? I went diving, digging, and delving through drawers and shelves for the letter about the house. Maybe it wasn't such a bad idea. Eureka! After a few phone calls, it was arranged; I was going house shopping. I hadn't planned to actually purchase anything, just to have an interesting few days' change from present activities!

After planes, trains, and automobiles, I finally was in a rented car driving south from Barcelona, along the Mediterranean coastal road called the *autopista* headed toward Valencia. Just typing these words, I almost tremble with excitement at the memory of it! A mere ten hours previous, I had left the early morning fog and eternal drizzle of an English summer, and now I was dazzled by sunshine and the azure brilliance of the sea, sparkling far below the cliffs on my left.

Castellón Province of Spain

Masia Albadas is located in the mountains that hug the Mediterranean Sea up and down the eastern coast of Spain in the Castellón Province.

Our home in Spain

By midnight, I had reached the house in Masia Albadas, a small, mountain settlement on the eastern coast of Spain in the Castellón Province. Here, time almost stands still. It is an agricultural area: Mainly almonds and olives are grown, most of the work is done by hand, and bulls are venerated.

The home itself has bars on the windows and is situated on the very edge of a precipice that descends to a dry riverbed far below—both facts affording me slight uneasiness at first.

But I stayed for almost a week. I explored the area; marveled at the hypnotic appeal of the nearby Mediterranean; tasted the food; ate fish with eyes still intact; and was irrevocably, irreversibly, irretrievably, once and forever convinced that this spot was to play a part in our lives. I negotiated at length with the owner and came to an agreement over the terms of purchasing the house.

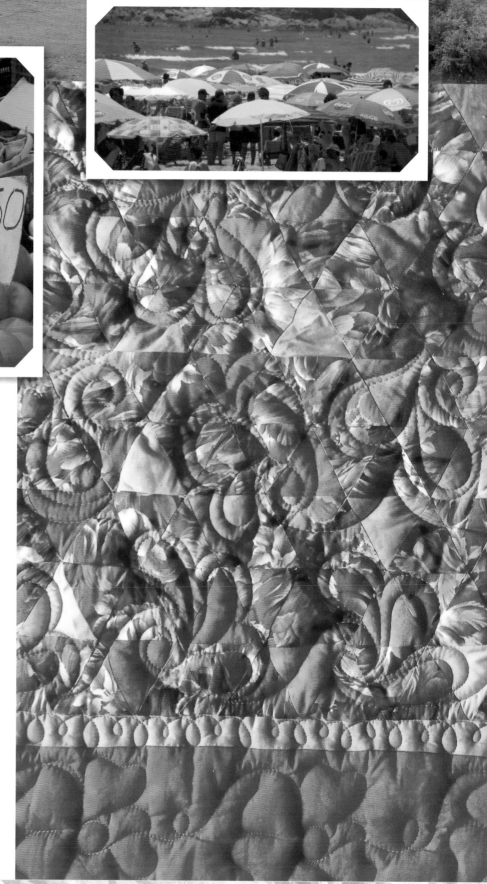

For years, the house at Albadas served as
a holiday spot for us, friends, and family.
In Cornwall we continued making pots,
running ceramic courses, and enter-
taining in what we finally converted to a
B&B. We opened a restaurant called The
Potter's Barn, featuring— you guessed
it—Mediterranean food. Finally, the rigors
of this routine became a bit much for
an aging couple, and when a local family
inquired about purchasing the property,
the decision was easy.

All roads led to Spain, it seemed. Moving
vans, channel crossings, and drives down
through France and across the Pyrenees
and beyond became familiar to us. In
Albadas, we had to establish a pottery,
construct a wood firing kiln, and enlarge
the main house, dealing with construction crews—all in a foreign language. The
details would fill volumes.

The Quilts

It was during this time that quilting entered my life. As with many of you, after I was stung by the cupid of quilts, nothing would ever be the same. I grew up sewing one thing or another: as a child, crocheting potholders; as a teenager, plowing through 4-H projects; as a college student, sewing for classmates to earn money; and upon the arrival of the first grandchild, doing English smocking and heirloom sewing. But none of it could challenge the effect quilting had on me.

As soon as the house at Albadas was more or less complete, I began to sew quilts. Day and night their patterns danced through my head—ballet, tango, foxtrot. I was as a woman possessed, possessed with colors and shapes and eye-catching effects. I dreamt in Technicolor triangles and saw quilts everywhere. Seth would wake up in the morning to find me cutting out fabric shapes and would retire to an empty bed at night. I couldn't stop.

Spain itself contributed greatly to the creative obsession. It is totally captivating, layer upon layer. The colors of Spain became the colors of quilts. Flowers, fields, rocks, fences, food, sunrises, sunsets all began to look like quilts.

Since I was very new to quiltmaking, the patterns in this book are simple and not terribly challenging technically. What I really want to address are questions of color and form. In Mediterranean light, colors are a bit better, the blue of the sky is a bit brighter, clouds are whiter, and sunsets are a bit more spectacular. (Mediterranean light is no secret, nor is it something new. Van Gogh was only one of many artists to seek out this southern light.) With most of the quilt projects

Magenta Magic (page 41) shaded by Spanish bougainvillea

comes some lesson in color—combinations, the use of it, intensities, warmth, and general tips and suggestions. I hope you find something helpful.

So, this book is first a collection of quilt and patchwork patterns inspired by the area, but also a glance into the wonderful place, its customs, its fiestas, its radiant fields of flowers, and even a few favorite recipes.

Please, enjoy. This book is most sincerely *From Spain with Love*.

A Few Thoughts on Color

Color is a vast and exciting subject that is often on the minds of many quilters. After all, the success of most of our quilts depends on wise, discerning color choices. In a sphere where there are neither true rights nor wrongs, it can all become confusing at times.

If you have basic quiltmaking skills, you will no doubt find the techniques used to make the quilts in this book well within your abilities. I hope that when constructing these comfortable quilts, you will take extra time to think about and reflect on your color choices. I talk about color throughout the book and offer hints with each project.

By all means, make choices with which you are comfortable, but if not necessarily stepping outside of your "box," do consider at least expanding its perimeters. I have presented a few color concepts throughout the book that, if absorbed and used to your advantage, can bring extra life, excitement, and movement to your quilts.

Understanding Color

Just for fun, let's consider the essential and even esoteric qualities of color. Life, in all its forms, is dependent upon the brilliant white light of the sun, the very same white light from which all colors come. I'm sure you have seen rays of sunshine pass through a prism or crystal and split into rainbows of color. In ways beyond my understanding, sunlight hits our atmosphere, splits, and splatters itself to surround us with the colors of nature.

The color wheel, a basic tool for quilters and artists alike, gives us a graphic way to represent all these colors. It basically lays out, in circular fashion, the colors in the order they appear when white light is split. As with all things created, there are absolutes and order that govern color and dictate the way in which colors interact with each other. It is by no means my intent to impose any "rules" of usage, but once armed with some basic "color truths," one is much more apt to make pleasing choices—to create color schemes that enliven and bring movement to the creation.

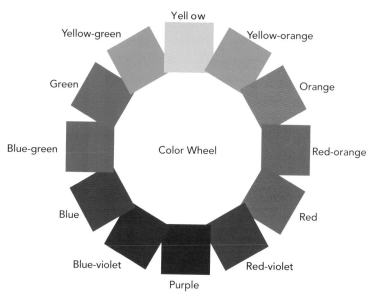

The color wheel

 I don't advocate carrying a color wheel around when making fabric choices. We all need to exercise artistic license and intuition in creating a pleasing palette. But sometimes when you're at a loss as to color choices, it's good to refer back to the indisputable basics of the color wheel.

Breaking up white light gives us the *primary colors*—red, yellow, and blue. Between these are the *secondary colors*—orange, green, and purple.

Detail of *The Pomegranate Path* (full quilt on page 29)

Detail of *Colors of Spain* (full quilt on page 37)

The gentle green of grass recedes; red poppy "pops."

For more about the use of secondary colors and to see a full view of *The Pomegranate Path*, see page 29.

Colors that lie next to each other on the wheel—*analogous colors*— share components (for example, orange is created by contributions from both red and yellow, the two colors lying at either side of orange). When placed together, they can form opulent harmony. Check out the use of red, yellow, and orange in *Colors of Spain* (page 35).

Basic colors have basic traits: Red is the hottest of all colors and suggests excitement. Yellow is the most prominent. There was an emperor of China who would be clothed only in yellow garments, no doubt to emphasize his supreme power—a small bit of yellow goes a long way. Blue is cool and calming; nothing is more peaceful than a tranquil blue sea. Green also is peaceful, but it has a wonderful receding quality and exists in this capacity in our natural surroundings.

Actually, there are many lessons about color to be learned by observing nature. In the Spanish countryside, the two main colors of the world are grass and leaf green, and sky blue. All else appears in front of this background. It is probably no accident that these two colors are easiest on the eyes. Green, as mentioned, especially appears to recede, allowing all other colors to take prominence. This is certainly a principle that can be carried into quiltmaking. I used it in the *In Spanish Fields* quilt (page 12). The brilliant red-orange poppies show off in front of the receding green background, just as they do in the fields of Spain.

Detail of *In Spanish Fields* (full quilt on page 12)

This quilt also makes use of a color scheme that consists of several shades and variations of two basic hues used in combination. The background of grasses is represented by many different shades of two main colors, green and gold. When you look closely at a field of wild grass, it is not difficult to see this endless variation of shades.

Using color schemes that feature and combine several shades and variations of one color can also create style, life, and interest in a quilt. I've labeled it "theme and variations" in the *Magenta Magic* quilt (page 41), and you can read more about it in that section.

Detail of *Magenta Magic* (full quilt on page 44)

The magentas, purples, and pinks all work well together in this quilt. Part of the reason for this brings us to another important concept—the idea of using fabrics of the same or very similar *intensity* within a single quilt.

Matching intensity matters a great deal in choosing your quilt fabrics, and it is a principle that features prominently in my quilts. Most of the projects in this book use relatively high-intensity color fabrics. For example, the "sun" quilts, *Music of the Dawn* (page 46) and *Seasons of Sunsets* (page 66), celebrate the rising or setting of the sun at their most intense best. It would not do to include even a swatch of pastel in either of these quilts. In fact, I have used batiks instead of solids. I consider vibrant batiks essential wherever an exciting solid is required; they are so interesting and alive with movement.

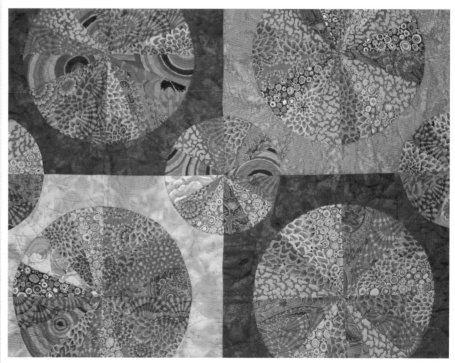

Detail of *Seasons of Sunsets* (full quilt on page 66)

Detail of *Music of the Dawn* (full quilt on page 46)

Of course, a quilt doesn't have to feature high-intensity colors to be successful. The level of intensity matters not at all, so long as all your fabrics are of the same intensity or nearly so.

I do want to mention the use of *complementary colors*, which lie opposite each other on the color wheel. When complementary colors appear together, each brings out the richness of its opposite. Have you ever wondered around Christmastime why red and green look so fantastic together? They are complementary colors and seem to belong together, each bringing out the best in the other. But don't forget, their intensities still have to match!

Yellow and purple—another set of perfect complementary colors

I have just touched on a few very basic color facts. I don't like the idea of getting too academic about color, because creating a quilt is an art that has to spring from the heart and imagination. Nonetheless, there are fundamental truths about colors that, if heeded, will improve the final result.

My husband is a potter who travels and lectures quite a bit. He talks and writes about what he terms the "language of shapes"—proportions within elementary shapes. He insists that even when a layperson looks at a shelf of pottery, his or her hand will go predictably to a pot that is proportionately correct! Similarly, your eye will be attracted to a quilt that has been created with sympathy and considerate attention to color.

With most of the quilt projects in this book, you will find short lessons and hints about the color ideas used in that particular quilt. Think of these as starting points from which you can grow schemes and combinations of your own. Even if you don't plan to construct each quilt, it might profit you to read through the introductions and lessons, just to expand your repertoire of color knowledge.

TIP

A design wall is a most effective tool for placing your colors where you want them. It does not have to be an entire wall; a 3-foot by 3-foot area is a good start. As you get more comfortable using the design wall, it can expand to an area large enough for an entire quilt to be displayed. To "build" the wall, simply cut a piece of cotton felt or cotton batting to the desired size and thumbtack it to a wall near your sewing machine. Keep it easily accessible. Your quilt pieces, blocks, or whatever can be placed wherever you want, and they will stick to the cotton wall. Stand back (very important) and look, change the position of anything that doesn't look or feel right, and then stand back and look again. In this manner, you can play with the pieces of the quilt, move them around—in short, design. It's like seeing into the future at a point where you can still change the outcome. I highly recommend it!

In Spanish Fields

Finished quilt size: 55″ × 75″
Finished block size: 10″ × 10″

Made by Roberta Cardew
and machine quilted by
Bobbi Lang.

You simply cannot think of Spanish fields without seeing bright orange, even brighter red-orange, and brilliant red. I know that poppies grow all over southern Europe and many other parts of the world as well, but if the poppies of Spain are not the best, they are at least way up there.

Also way up there, high in the clouds about 45 minutes away from our home, is a fortified town called Morella. In the spring of the year, its surrounding walls offer a perfect vantage point from which to see the fields around Morella, which are ablaze with millions and millions of poppies, or so it would seem. This trail of red continues along roadways and across fields throughout the entire province. As I mentioned, they only bloom in the spring, so for the rest of the year, a quilt is needed!

Color Lesson

As this quilt demonstrates, green is a relaxing color that recedes naturally into the background. It provides the perfect backdrop for highlighting a special feature—red and orange poppies, in this case—as nature intended.

The colors in the quilt represent the different grasses of the field. Grass greens—the predominant color—are interspersed with tans and golds that represent the dried grasses. The rich brown is just a splash here and there for depth.

Green is the obvious choice here, since grass is being depicted, but the color can be used under any circumstance with the same receding, relaxed effect.

You can approach making this quilt with a relaxed attitude as well. Nothing about it is very disciplined or too exact. It's for fun.

Morella

Built in the thirteenth century on top of the ruins of even earlier Roman fortresses, the town of Morella is situated over 3,000 feet above sea level. Morella can be seen from miles away. It is still a thriving town, much given to the arts. The beautiful fourteenth-century church of Santa Maria is a jewel of Gothic excellence. The church still serves the community, and every six years since 1673, a statue of the Virgin Maria has been carried up to the church in a procession of grand Spanish style.

The charm of Morella's maze of narrow, winding streets and alleys is immense. The medieval stone wall surrounding the town unbroken for almost two miles is wide enough for houses to be built upon and has a number of descending spiral ledges functioning as walkways. They connect the narrow rectangular openings where archers of ancient times did their defending. I use them to gaze out upon...yes, fields of poppies!

In Spanish Fields

Materials

Yardage is based on fabric that measures 42" wide.

- Varying shades of green, tan, and gold* (batiks, small-scale prints, and solids): 19–21 fat quarters (18" × 20"–22") or ¼-yard pieces
- Rich brown fabric: 1 fat quarter or ¼ yard
- Slightly darker green for the borders: ¾ yard
- Red batik for poppies: ⅜ yard
- Red-orange batik for poppies: ⅜ yard
- Orange batik for poppies: ⅜ yard
- Solid black fabric for the poppy centers: ⅛ yard
- Fabric for backing: 4¾ yards**
- Fabric for binding: ⅝ yard
- Batting: 63" × 83"
- Fusible web: 1¾ yards
- Template plastic or paper
- Fabric glue

*Note: The greens will be predominant, so you will need fewer fat quarters of the golds and tans.

**Note: Because you will be attaching the poppies with a tacking stitch in black thread, it is best to choose a fabric such as a small-scale print that will "hide" these little stitches. I used a green tiny print but was tempted to use red.

Cutting

GRASS FABRIC:

Cut the fat quarters the long way (parallel to the 20″–22″ side) into strips varying between 1″ and 2″ wide. Cut fewer of the 1″ and 2″ widths and more of the "in-between" widths. You will need at least 275 strips total. Note: If you are using straight ¼-yard pieces, cut them in half to create 2 pieces approximately 9″ × 20″–22″, and then cut into strips 20″–22″ long.

BORDER FABRIC:

Cut 7 strips 3″ × width of the fabric; join them end to end with diagonal seams (see Quilting Basics, page 71).

POPPY FABRICS:

See Making the Poppies, page 16.

To keep your cut strips organized and separated by color, hang them on a wooden rack made for drying clothes or herbs.

Preparing the Templates

From paper or template plastic, cut out 3 rectangular templates in the following sizes:

- Rectangle A: 5½″ × 10½″
- Rectangle B: 5½″ × 6½″
- Rectangle C: 5½″ × 4½″

If you use paper, make 5 copies of each.

Making the Blocks

JOIN THE STRIPS

Sew together the fabric strips right sides together, along the long edges, to make a strip set 45″ wide. Repeat to make 8 strip sets 45″ × 20″–22″. Vary the fabrics as you go along to avoid placing the same fabric side by side. Add the gold and dark brown strips only every so often. Sew each seam in the opposite direction from the previous seam, like plowing a field, to prevent distortion. Press.

Note: You will probably have more strips than required to make the quilt this size, but the given number of different fabrics is required to achieve the variation in shades of color. Of course, you can use the extra strips to enlarge the quilt if you wish, depending on how economically you cut the rectangles.

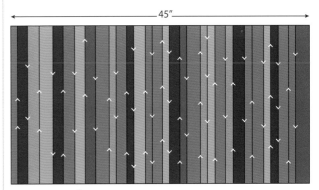

Sew strips together.

CUT OUT THE BLOCKS

Place your templates on your strip sets. Lay them at a slight angle to perpendicular, varying between approximately 5° and 15°. Vary the angles and slant the templates in different directions as shown. These strips represent the field grasses as they blow in the wind, so straight up-and-down grass is out! Cut 35 each of Rectangles A, B, and C.

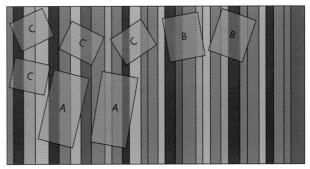

Place templates at varying angles and directions.

Note: If your templates are paper, pin and cut them out as you would the pieces of a garment. If using a plastic template and rotary cutter, be sure to have a fresh blade. Don't worry if things are not just exactly precise; there are no triangle points to position!

SEW THE BLOCKS

Note: Vary the direction of the slant of each adjoining rectangle as much as possible.

1. Sew 1 Rectangle B to 1 Rectangle C as shown. Press.

2. To these, sew 1 Rectangle A. Press.

3. Repeat to make 35 blocks 10½" × 10½".

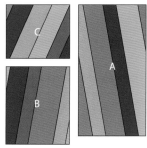

Sew the blocks.

Assembling the Quilt Top

When you arrange the blocks, try to keep the strips of "grass" in adjoining pieces leaning in different directions. This may not always be possible, but do your best!

1. To make a horizontal row, sew together 5 blocks side to side. Turn every other block upside down so that the small Rectangle C is alternately at the top and bottom of each block. Press.

2. Repeat to make a total of 7 rows.

3. Sew the rows together. Press.

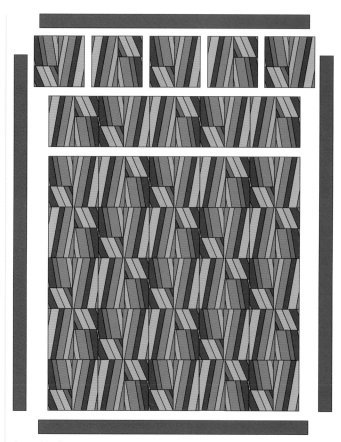

Assembly diagram

Making the Border

Refer to Quilting Basics (page 71) to make squared borders. The finished borders are 2½" wide.

Quilting

Refer to Quilting Basics (page 72) to layer and quilt your quilt.

This quilt was machine quilted in a simple meandering pattern with dark green thread, which pulls in the dark green of the border. You will attach the poppies after quilting.

Making the Poppies

This quilt features about 200 poppies, and they are so-o-o much fun. Make more or fewer to your taste. They are in 3 different colors and 3 different sizes. Trace and cut out the poppy and center template patterns on page 74.

1. Cut each of the 3 poppy fabrics in half lengthwise to make pieces approximately 13½" × 20"–22". Following the manufacturer's instructions, use fusible web to fuse the 2 halves of each color together right sides out.

2. Using the templates made from the patterns on page 74, cut out about 200 poppies from the fused fabrics. Vary the colors and the sizes. They do not need to be exact; in fact, it is better if they are not! Poppies are like snowflakes—no two are alike. You will probably get so good at cutting poppies that you won't even need a pattern.

3. Use the templates to cut out the black centers in 2 sizes. Match the center sizes to the poppy sizes and attach a center to each poppy with a drop of fabric glue.

4. Lay out the quilt and randomly place the poppies. Let them splash across the quilt. They can overlap, they can trail, and they can grow alone or in bunches. It's all up to you. Attach them to the quilt with fabric glue. Keep the glue away from the edges of the poppies so they will have a natural feel. Hopefully, they will fray just a bit over time.

5. When the glue is dry, use your sewing machine to make 4–5 tacking stitches in the middle of each poppy head with black thread. It won't be noticed and provides assurance that the poppies won't come off in the wash.

Finishing

The only thing remaining is to bind the quilt (see Quilting Basics, page 72), and it's finished. Poppies for all seasons!

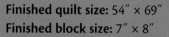

Searching for Sailboats

Finished quilt size: 54″ × 69″
Finished block size: 7″ × 8″

Made by Roberta Cardew and machine quilted
by Bobbi Lang.

Sailboats… is it even possible to describe the delight in sighting a sailboat, white sails gliding over a calm sea?

The sight of sailboats evokes an existence that includes relaxation, a certain calm and tranquility, a pleasurable satisfaction with life, an undeniable respite, and an easing of tensions that often happens when one is by the sea. Equally amazing is the thrill of watching for the sea to appear as we maneuver the hairpin curves on the drive from our home down to the Mediterranean coast in order to spend some time in the sand. In the marina at Oropesa del Mar, sailboats rock gently on the blue water.

All in all, sailboats certainly suggest feelings worth searching out. To be quite honest (don't laugh), I experience similar feelings when I put on marvelous music and sit down at the sewing machine! It's a superb feeling— it's how I felt making this quilt. Perhaps what we search for is right under our noses. No ruby slippers required!

This whimsical quilt should vaguely remind you of sailboats! Just search. Hint: The 2½″ border is made up of small, pieced "nautical flags," each one rotated 90° from the adjoining flag.

The quilt is made up of 42 identical blocks, each framed with a 1″-wide lattice strip. The pieces are easily cut using 4 templates, and the blocks are easily assembled. So relax—there's no rush.

Color Lesson

You're sure to enjoy searching out fabrics in sailor colors—basically red, blue, and gold. (This is a classic triadic color scheme, made up of three colors equidistant from each other on the color wheel.) Include touches of white, but avoid fabric containing very much bright white; off-white and creams are preferable.

Because this is a scrappy quilt, you can use fabrics from your stash, purchased fat quarters, or a combination. The important thing is that the shades blend well and are of similar intensity.

The pieced border representing nautical flags, also in these colors, is great fun. Best of all will be seeing a child in your life sleeping peacefully beneath this quilt, perhaps dreaming of sailboats.

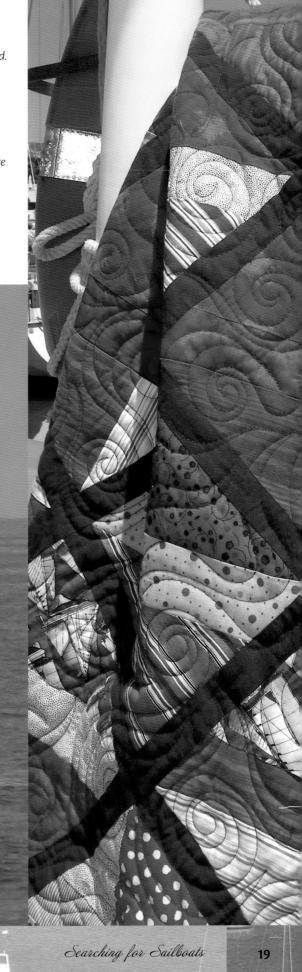

Materials

Yardage is based on fabric that measures 42" wide.

- Various solids and prints in shades of red, white, blue, and gold (not yellow) for the blocks and border: I used 18–20 fat quarters.
- Navy or royal blue solid fabric for the lattice strips and binding: 1¾ yards
- Fabric for the backing: 3⅝ yards
- Batting: 62" × 77"
- Template plastic or paper

Cutting

Cut strips on the crosswise grain, from selvage to selvage.

FROM THE NAVY SOLID FABRIC:

Cut 13 strips 1½" wide; subcut into 49 strips 8½" long for the vertical lattice strips.

Cut 12 strips 1½" wide for the horizontal lattice strips. Join end to end as needed with diagonal seams (see Quilting Basics, page 71); subcut into 8 strips, each 54" long.

 I recommend using spray sizing as you press; it will help to keep the bias edges of the triangles from stretching out of shape.

Making the Blocks

Template patterns are on pages 74–76.

1. Trace and cut out the template patterns A (the hull of the boat), B and C (the sail), and D (the keel) from template plastic or paper.

2. Use the templates to cut out a total of 42 of each shape from the block fabrics. Make sure to cut some of every fabric in every shape. Save extra fabrics for the pieced border.

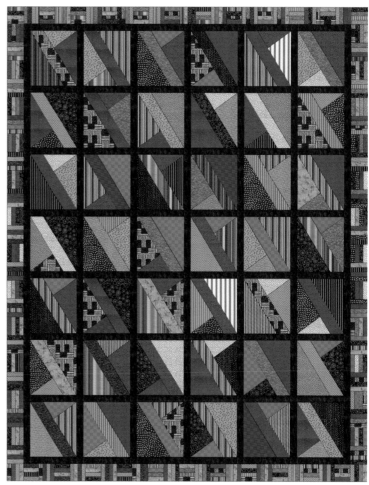

Searching for Sailboats

 Important! When working with block pieces A, B, C, and D—whether paper pieces, templates, or fabric—keep them right side up. Do not flip pattern pieces over; they will not fit together unless they are kept right side up.

3. Stitch 1 piece A to 1 piece B. Press.

4. Stitch 1 piece C to the A/B unit, and finally stitch 1 piece D to the edge of C. Press, using spray sizing.

5. Repeat to make 42 blocks.

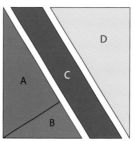

Assemble each block.

Assembling the Quilt Top

1. To make a horizontal row, select 6 blocks and 7 lattice strips 8½″ × 1½″. Sew a lattice strip to the left longer side of a block. Continue sewing the row as shown, alternating the blocks and lattice strips. Rotate every other block 180° so that the small section of the sail is at the top of one block and at the bottom of the next. Press.

Assemble the rows.

2. Repeat to make a total of 7 rows. Press.
3. Use the 54″ lattice strips between the 7 horizontal rows of blocks. The strips will be a little too long but will allow extra at each end and can be trimmed later for a straight edge.
4. Sew a long lattice strip to the top edge of the first row of blocks.
5. Sew together the remaining lattice strips and rows of blocks, alternating between strips and blocks and ending with a lattice strip. Press.
6. With a ruler and rotary cutter, trim the sides of the quilt even.

Making the Border

Now for the fun! No strict instructions here. The border, made to resemble a collection of little nautical flags, will give the final "sailor" touch to the quilt.

1. Cut narrow strips from each of the remaining red, blue, and gold block fabrics. They do not have to be the same width, but graduated from ¾″ wide to about 1½″ wide. Sew together the strips randomly, side to side, until you have a 3″-wide strip set. Press, using spray sizing. Note: The length of the cut strips will not matter, because it depends on the sizes of your remaining fabrics. Just make enough strip sets to yield 108–110 squares 3″ × 3″.
2. Cut the strip sets into 3″ × 3″ pieces to make a total of 108–110 squares.
3. Stitch together the squares into a long strip, rotating each square 90° from the previous one. Construct 2 strips of flags to equal the side measurements of the quilt for the side borders.

4. Sew the side borders to the sides of the quilt edges (see Quilting Basics, page 71). If the corners don't come out exactly right, no problem—just trim off the excess of the border. Press.

5. Repeat for the top and bottom borders, constructing 2 strips equal to the width of the quilt, including the side borders. Press.

Finishing

Refer to Quilting Basics (page 72) to layer, quilt, and bind your quilt.

Assembly diagram

Spanish Fish Stew

Another great pleasure of being by the sea is eating seafood! In Spain there are countless rice-based dishes, such as paella, that use all sorts of fish and shellfish. Here's a stew recipe—just fish, no rice—that I've developed from scratch over the years, inspired by those great Spanish dishes. It can be made with or without shellfish, but shellfish do add a little *je ne sais quoi*.

Please try this stew and pretend you're by the sea.

Stew base

- 6 tablespoons olive oil
- 1 large onion, peeled and chopped
- 1 red and 1 green bell pepper, chopped
- 3 carrots, peeled and chopped
- Lots of garlic (at least 5 cloves—don't worry; it totally tames as it cooks!)
- 2 large cans chopped tomatoes
- 3 cups water
- 2 cups dry white wine
- 4 fish stock cubes or 6 tablespoons of fish sauce (usually sold in Asian foods section of the supermarket)
- 3 star anise
- 1 orange, juice and rind
- 3 large bay leaves
- Begin with 1 teaspoon of each of the following; adjust to taste later:
  - Dried basil
  - Dried oregano
  - Dried thyme
  - Red pepper flakes
  - Dried or fresh chopped parsley
  - Sea salt

Place a large soup pot over medium heat. Add oil, then chopped vegetables. Sweat the vegetables until they are soft, not browned. Add all remaining ingredients and simmer for about 45 minutes over low heat. While the soup base is simmering, prepare the fish.

Fish

2–2½ pounds of fish. A mixture of two or three different kinds is best; I like cod or halibut and salmon. Try to get thick fillets.

Shellfish, cleaned (optional: your choice—tiny shrimp, large shrimp with shells on or off, mussels, clams)
- ½ sliced onion
- 1 teaspoon peppercorns
- 2 bay leaves

Place all ingredients except the shellfish in a saucepan and add water to cover. Poach over medium heat just until fish begins to flake (not very long). Set aside to cool. When cool enough to handle, drain and reserve liquid. Carefully remove skin, and break the fish into roughly 2″-square pieces. It is good to have generous pieces of fish in the stew. Put the fish back into the strained poaching liquid and set aside to wait until soup base has finished simmering.

When the soup has reduced, taste and adjust herbs and seasonings. If you wish, add 2 or 3 additional cloves of chopped garlic. Add fish, poaching liquid, and shellfish if using.

Gently simmer on low heat for 10–15 minutes. Remove orange peel, star anise, and bay leaf if desired. I actually like to leave the bay leaf in—a nice touch. (If you used mussels, make sure they have opened, and discard any that haven't.)

To serve, sprinkle with fresh parsley or a fresh sprig of thyme. Dried will do in a pinch.

Make the soup a day or two ahead if you can; it only improves with time (within reason!). Of course, keep it refrigerated. When reheating, make sure it is good and hot. Wow!

Into the Courtyard

Finished quilt size: 67½″ × 82½″
Finished block size: 7½″ × 7½″

Made by Roberta Cardew and machine quilted by Bobbi Lang.

The courtyard of our house in Spain was an addition we made after making a driving trip into France searching out a wondrous place, Rennes le Château. Seth was in hot pursuit of historic remnants and evidences of the Knights Templar. I got to navigate! The château and cathedral are situated in the foothills of the French Pyrenees, lovely old historic structures for Seth and a forgotten courtyard garden for me, walled by crumbling, ivy-covered stones. There was a place to sit under an old tree and listen as water trickled from a peaceful fountain. An unworldly quiet reigned there—and there, the idea of a walled courtyard at Albadas was hatched. I felt that I wouldn't mind capturing this feeling and taking it home. And that is exactly what happened.

Back home, the work soon began. Seth modeled a face of Flora, Roman goddess of flowers, springtime, and (ahem) fertility, which was set into a corner fountain. Flowers were brought in, and the jacaranda tree encouraged to put forth its fragrant lavender blue flowers. A floor of handmade terra cotta tiles was laid in the pattern of *octagonal con taco*, which means octagonal tiles joined at the corners with little, rotated

Color Lesson

When you choose your fabrics, select colors that befriend each other and also are of a similar intensity. The intensity here should be high, because with so much tile-colored background fabric, the floral prints have to carry the quilt. This quilt is such a delight to make, and, finished, it is a very elegant piece.

squares. The final touch was a pair of reclaimed antique carved doors.

This beautiful courtyard had to have a quilt! The quilt is a traditional snowball pattern, but I was only thinking octagonal tiles when making it. The corner joining squares represent the masses of flowers in the courtyard, and the background "snowballs" are made from a terra cotta–colored fabric to represent the tiles…of course! The quilt is made from only one shape in two sizes: a small square and a larger one. Everything happens in the small floral print squares, so have fun choosing your fabrics.

The Pyrenees

Another very nice thing about Spain is that France is just on the other side of the Pyrenees Mountains. Foreboding, dark, and enigmatic, they are in themselves reward enough to venture a crossing. At first, in the meadows of the lower slopes on the Spanish side, cows graze, bells around their necks ringing out enchanting melodies. But past the cows and up into the clouds and beyond, the scene changes, and shivers travel down your spine. Cascading waterfalls thunder into mountain lakes, goats somehow stay glued to rugged outcrops of rock, and if you happen to catch a spring snow and become engulfed in a whirlwind of giant flakes, you'll feel yourself inside a Currier and Ives. Total beguilement.

Soon the descent into the gentleness of western France plunges you into another atmosphere altogether. There are still mountains, but lower and green and wildflower carpeted.

Into the Courtyard

Materials

Yardage is based on fabric that measures 42" wide.

- Terra cotta-colored fabric for the large squares: 3⅛ yards
- 8 different floral fabrics (Fabrics A through H) for the small squares: ⅓ yard of each
- Floral fabric (Fabric Z) for the border, binding, and small squares around the perimeter of the "courtyard": 2⅞ yards
- Fabric for the backing: 5 yards
- Batting: 75" × 90"
- Fabric marking pen with disappearing ink

My favorite marking pen is the Sewline Fabric Pencil. It makes clean, clear, precise lines, and it is easily removed with moisture. It enables you to draw a very thin line that stays in place until you decide to dampen it.

Cutting

Cut strips on the crosswise grain, from selvage to selvage.

TERRA COTTA FABRIC:

Cut 13 strips 8" wide; subcut into 63 squares 8" × 8" to represent terra cotta tiles

8 FLORAL FABRICS A THROUGH H:

Cut 2 strips 3¼" wide; subcut into 24 small squares 3¼" × 3¼" from each fabric for the block corners. (Keep the different floral fabrics separate and label the stacks.)

FLORAL FABRIC Z:

Cut 8 strips 8" wide for the border. Join them end to end with diagonal seams (see Quilting Basics, page 71).

Cut 5 strips 3¼" wide; subcut into 60 squares 3¼" × 3¼" for the Z block corners around the perimeter of the quilt top. (Label the stack.)

Making the Blocks

Make 63 blocks.

DRAW A STITCHING GUIDELINE

You will be sewing a small square to each corner of the larger squares in order to create triangles at the corners. A stitching guideline will help you to stitch accurately. If you feel sufficiently experienced at this process, you can skip this step.

There will be 24 squares of each fabric A through H, and 60 squares of fabric Z. Using a disappearing ink fabric pen, carefully draw a diagonal line from corner to corner on each 3¼" square.

Draw stitching guideline.

> **TIP**
>
> To draw a very accurate line, place the fabric square on a gridded cutting mat with the corners lined up on a diagonal line. Lay a traditional ruler (not a quilter's ruler, which is too thick) along the diagonal line of the cutting mat to draw a true corner-to-corner line.

SEW THE SQUARES

1. Position 1 small square at each corner of the 8″ terra cotta squares, right sides together. The Fabric A through H and Fabric Z squares must be positioned exactly as shown in the assembly diagram (page 28). Later, when you assemble the blocks, each corner triangle must join 3 matching floral fabric triangles.

2. Stitch together the squares along your drawn guidelines.

3. Trim off the outer corners of the small squares and the large square behind them ¼″ outside the seam.

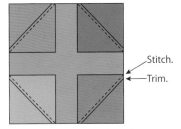

Stitch.
Trim.

Place, stitch, and trim the 3¼″ corner squares.

4. Repeat to make 63 blocks.

> **TIP**
>
> The stitching guideline is at most ¹⁄₁₆″ wide, maybe less. It is a subtle task, but if you stitch just to the outside of the line, when you press the tip of the squares outward to form triangles, their points will be sure to reach the corner of the block. This is a distance almost too small to see, but the effort has excellent results! In any case, do not stitch at all to the inner side of the drawn line.

5. Fold open the small squares at the stitching lines and press. This achieves the triangle needed at each corner. Use spray sizing on the bias corners as you press.

Assembling the Quilt Top

As mentioned, the quilt blocks have to be sewn together so that matching floral fabric triangles meet at each block "intersection." It is helpful if you can lay the blocks out, either on a design wall or on a clean floor or large table. If you don't have enough space, work a row or two at a time and refer to the assembly diagram as you go. It will help to number the rows 1 through 9.

1. Sew together 7 blocks to make the top row (Row 1). Repeat to make a total of 9 rows. The top and bottom rows will have Fabric Z triangles along one long edge and on each end. In each of the remaining rows, the Fabric Z triangles will be on the ends. These triangles will match and blend into the borders.

2. Beginning with Rows 1 and 2, sew together the rows in order.

Assembly diagram

Borders and Finishing

Refer to Quilting Basics (page 71) to attach borders and to layer, quilt, and bind the quilt using the remaining Fabric Z.

The Pomegranate Path

Finished quilt size: 60″ × 52″

Made by Roberta Cardew and machine quilted by Bobbi Lang.

Although the pomegranate has become popular in the United States, in our area of Spain, it is held in no esteem whatsoever. Small pomegranate trees grow wild and dot the countryside. Their striking, almost iridescent orange blossoms mature slowly into swollen fruits of brilliant red, which hang enticingly from the tree only to become overripe and fall to the ground. The exotic plump scarlet seeds return to nature. It was the intense color of the flowers, fruits, and seeds that inspired this quilt.

Now let us wander down the Pomegranate Path! It is an easy walk from the courtyard to the pomegranate tree, and it is an easy job to make this fun quilt. Because you needn't worry about exact cutting or matching corners or points, you can turn yourself loose to choose colors. Such great fun!

Color Lesson

I'll go so far as to say that the appeal of this quilt hangs totally upon color. I chose the bright orange batik as the dominant, or featured, color because it echoes the color of the pomegranate blossom. The other obvious choice was to use browns and tans to mirror the earth tones of the pathway. Fine, except it is not enough color and lacks life.

At this stage, auditioning fabrics on a design wall (see page 11) helps make good decisions intuitive. Sometimes, though, it is good to use a more academic approach to back up the intuition. Looking at the color wheel (page 8), you will notice that the secondary colors to either side of red are orange and purple. Simply put, this means that both orange and purple are made up of half red, which makes them good companions. So I chose a strong purple batik as the other featured color.

I'll mention intensity as well. It's best to choose colors of similar intensities to use in a quilt. For instance, even though it is in the purple family, pale lavender would not have worked with the intense orange of the pomegranate blossom; the strength of the purple had to match the strength of the orange.

One more hint: For the four prints—the supporting colors—I chose fabrics with bits of purple and/or orange in the print. This helped to visually pull the whole quilt together. Unity can also be helped by using a well-considered border. I think that we too often minimize the importance of the border. It is not an afterthought, but a finishing touch. Borders can contribute in various ways to the overall feel of the quilt. Here I dispensed with the border altogether because everything I tried suggested a fence. Instead, I pieced together several strips from the quilt fabrics to form a wide binding. It works!

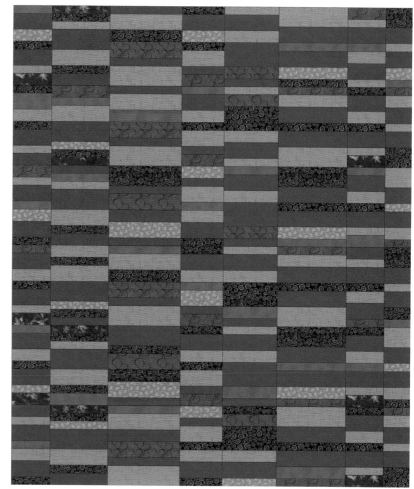

The Pomegranate Path

Materials

Yardage is based on fabric that measures 40"–42" wide.

- Strong orange batik: ⅝ yard
- Deep purple batik: ⅝ yard
- Camel-colored batik: ⅝ yard
- Rich brown batik: ⅝ yard
- 4 print fabrics, each containing some of the orange or purple: ⅝ yard of each
- Backing fabric: 3½ yards
- Batting: 68" × 60"

Note: The binding will be made from a combination of all of the above fabrics.

Cutting

Cut strips lengthwise, with the grain, parallel to the selvages.

Cut 1 strip 4½″ wide from each of 5 fabrics and 2 strips 4½″ wide from each of 3 fabrics and set aside for the extra-wide binding.

Cut the remainder of all the fabrics into strips of varying widths between 1″ and 2½″, with most strips falling within the 1½″ to 2″ range. They do not have to be measured, just so long as there is a good assortment of widths.

TIP You will have a great many 22½″ +/– strips, and assembling the quilt will be easier if you keep them separated by color and print. Quilt racks or racks for drying clothes make great stands for holding and organizing fabric strips.

Making the Quilt Top

SEW THE STRIPS

1. Sew together strips along the long sides in random order. Try to alternate batiks with prints. Sew each seam in the opposite direction from the last, up and down the rows, like plowing a field. This prevents the strips from becoming distorted. Continue piecing strips until you have a strip set that measures approximately 62″ wide. Press.

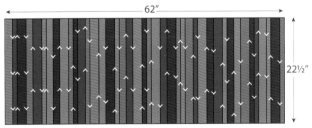

Stitching directions

2. Repeat Step 1 to make a total of 3 randomly ordered strip sets, each measuring approximately 62″ × 22½″. Remember— this quilt is not about exactness, but about color.

CUT THE STRIP SETS APART

Using a ruler and rotary cutter, crosscut the 3 strip sets into a total of 8 pieced strips 62″ wide, as shown. These 62″ strips will each make a row across the width of the quilt. To keep the strips organized, put a sticky note on each strip as it is cut, noting its size. Note: You will have leftovers.

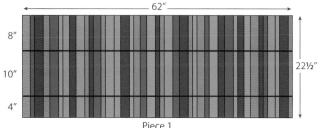

62"

8"

10"

4"

22½"

Piece 1

Cut into 3 pieces: 8", 10", and 4" wide.

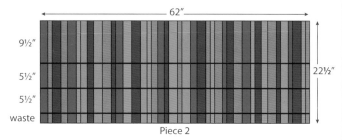

62"

9½"

5½"

5½"

waste

22½"

Piece 2

Cut into 3 pieces: 9½", 5½", and 5½" wide.

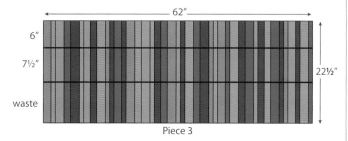

62"

6"

7½"

waste

22½"

Piece 3

Cut into 2 pieces: 6" and 7½" wide.

Crosscut strip sets.

SEW THE ROWS

1. Sew together the 8 pieces 62" wide, along the long sides. Begin at the top row with a 5½" piece, and sew it to an 8" piece. Proceed row by row with the remaining pieces in this order: 10", 6", 7½", 9½", 5½", ending with a 4" piece at the bottom. Again, sew each seam in the opposite direction from the last. This technique is required to keep the final piece square.

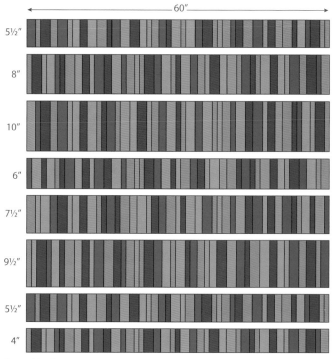

60"

5½"

8"

10"

6"

7½"

9½"

5½"

4"

Assembly diagram

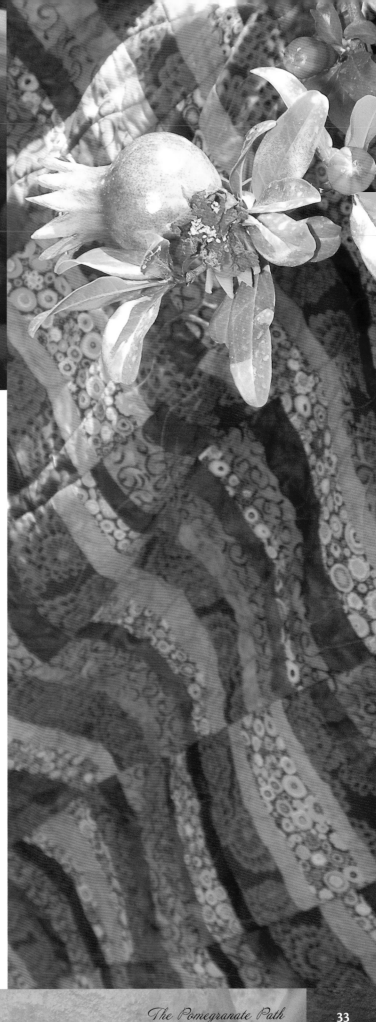

TIP

When assembling the pieces, take care that strips of the same color do not lie directly above and below each other. There is 2″ of leeway at the outer edges of the quilt top, which gives you room to shift the rows back and forth a bit. The other remedy is to turn one piece upside down to give a different order of colors. Play with it a bit as you go along.

2. Once the 8 pieces have been sewn together, trim the edges to square the quilt to approximately 60½″ × 52½″. Press the seams in the same direction, then press well on the right side to prepare for quilting.

Finishing and Binding

Refer to Quilting Basics (page 72) to layer and quilt your quilt.

To make the binding, sew together end to end the 4½″-wide strips of varying fabrics used in the quilt. Alternate colors as you go along. Press the binding in half lengthwise and attach a wide binding to the quilt, following the instructions in Quilting Basics (page 72) but rather than using a ¼″-wide seam to attach the binding, use a ⅝″-wide seam.

Angel's Pomegranate Seed Salad

In Spain, I know only two people who eat pomegranates. Angel (her real name) and her Belgian husband live very close to the earth without the benefit of running water or electricity in their little one-room house that Jack built, high, high in the mountains. Lack of amenities does not interfere with Angel's cooking. It is superb! The offerings from her gardens, bushes, and trees make up the majority of their vegetarian diet. It is her beautiful and delicious Pomegranate Seed Salad that stands out in my mind. It's a bit fussy to make but well worth the trouble!

Note that this not a formal recipe: Adjust the amount of each ingredient to your taste. Make as much as you and yours can eat!

- 1 large red onion
- Balsamic vinegar
- Pomegranates (2 or more)
- Good quality olive oil
- Salt to taste

Finely chop half of the red onion and put it in a serving bowl. Add balsamic vinegar just to barely cover. Let this marinate while peeling and separating seeds from the pomegranates. (Do this over a bowl to catch the juice.) Add seeds and juice to the onion and vinegar. Add a shake of salt to begin; add more only if your taste strongly calls for it. Finish with a few splashes of olive oil. Again, the amount can be adjusted to your taste. What needs to come through is the sweet, mild taste of the marinated onion and the zing, bam, boom of the pomegranate. Toss well. The dish only improves as it waits to be eaten.

Colors of Spain

Finished quilt size: 69¾" × 79½"

Made by Roberta Cardew and machine quilted by Bobbi Lang.

Red and yellow—these colors are tied up in the warmth and excitement of Spain itself. Red is the color of some of Spain's favorite things, not the least of which is the bullfight! The bull's eyes are always painted red in posters, the matador's cape is red, and red is the color of the neck scarves of all who run each year with the bulls through the streets of Pamplona. When it's time for bull-related celebrations, red and yellow flags are strung across the main streets of every village in our province.

However, a subject infinitely more interesting to me is food! I would say that food is enjoyed more in Spain than anywhere else I've ever been, and without a doubt, the red tomato is the star of the *cucina*. It's featured in soups, salads, tarts, sauces, and gazpachos. But the ultimate treat is pan tostado—wonderful, open-textured bread (baked daily in wood-fired ovens in every village throughout the area) that is sliced, toasted, rubbed with a clove of fresh garlic, then rubbed again with a juicy tomato cut in half, and finally drizzled with olive oil. Oh, I can't describe the taste; the words have not yet been invented! (For two delicious tomato-based recipes with taste explosion, turn to pages 39–40.)

This quilt is based on the equilateral triangle (each angle of the triangle is 60°). The technique used is assembling a triangle within a triangle (referred to in the project instructions as "TnT"). There are 1,380 small triangles in all. But don't despair—they go together quickly, and it's wonderful fun watching the quilt grow!

Color Lesson

Red, orange, and yellow are the hottest things going on the color wheel. Anytime two primary colors are used together, an eye-catching effect is produced. It is further enhanced when the secondary color falling between them is incorporated—in this instance, orange. In addition to being eye catching, these three particular colors exude exceptional warmth and produce a visual flaming up of the analogous orange lying between yellow and red.

Of the 1,380 triangles in the quilt, 1,035 are of the same fabric. Choose a small-scale, intensely hued print that has the main colors you want to feature: in this quilt, red, yellow, and orange. The print is cut into triangles and reassembled for a very interesting effect. The remaining triangles are divided into three solid colors; in this instance, batiks are a good choice because of their intense colors—what this quilt is all about.

Colors of Spain

Materials

Yardage is based on fabrics that measure 42" wide.

- Featured print fabric: 4½ yards
- 3 solid fabrics (red, gold-tinted yellow, and orange): ¾ yard each
- Inner border fabric: ½ yard
- Outer border fabric: 1⅝ yards
- Backing fabric: 4⅞ yards
- Binding fabric: ⅝ yard
- Batting: 78" × 87"
- Quilter's ruler with 60° marked angles

Cutting

Cut strips on the crosswise grain, from selvage to selvage.

Print fabric: Cut 50 strips 3" wide; subcut into 1,035 triangles, as described on page 37.

Red, yellow, and orange solid fabrics: Cut 6 strips 3" wide; subcut into 115 triangles of each fabric.

Inner border fabric: Cut 8 strips 1½" wide; join end to end with diagonal seams (see Quilting Basics, page 71).

Outer border fabric: Cut 9 strips 5½" wide; join end to end with diagonal seams.

Making the Quilt Top

CUT THE TRIANGLES

To cut the equilateral triangles, line up a 3"-wide fabric strip on a large cutting mat. Lay a ruler with 60° marked angles at the baseline, and use a rotary cutter to cut the triangle sides. Rotate the ruler to cut the next triangle. (The triangle point will be 60° as well.) The triangles will be 3½" at the base and on both sides. Cut 21 triangles per strip for a total of 1,035 print triangles and 345 solid triangles.

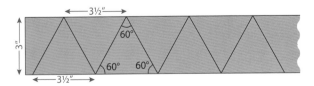

Cut equilateral triangles.

ASSEMBLE THE TNTS (TRIANGLES WITHIN TRIANGLES)

1. Select 4 triangles—3 print and 1 solid—and sew a print triangle to each side of the solid triangle. Press the seams toward the center triangle, using spray sizing. This will help stabilize the bias edges as you work on further assembly.

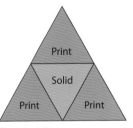

Create a TnT.

2. Repeat to make 345 TnTs.

SEW THE ROWS

1. Lay out the blocks on your design wall, randomly placing the solid triangles in a pleasing fashion. Use 23 TnTs for each of the 15 rows. Make sure to distribute the solid-colored triangles as much as possible throughout the quilt, not concentrating the colors into one spot. While laying it out, also be sure to orient the TnTs so they can be sewn together into rows as shown in Step 3. There will an extra ½ triangle at the end of each row. When the quilt top is finished, the excess will be trimmed off, leaving a perfectly squared quilt.

2. To stitch together 2 TnTs, flip 1 upside down and place it on top of a second TnT, right sides together. Stitch them together along the right side, as shown. Press.

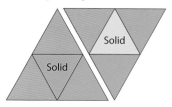

Stitch together 2 TnTs.

3. Repeat Step 2 with 21 additional TnTs to complete the row. Alternate the position of the solid-colored triangles—pointing up, the next pointing down—and vary their colors as you go along. Make a total of 15 rows. Press.

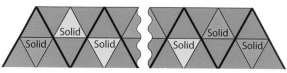

Assembly diagram for rows

JOIN THE ROWS AND TRIM

1. Sew the rows together. Press.

2. Using a large cutting mat, long ruler, and rotary cutter, trim off the extra half-triangles at the row ends to square up the quilt top.

ATTACH THE BORDERS

There are 2 squared borders—a narrow inner border and a wider outer border. Refer to Quilting Basics (page 71) to measure and attach the inner border; repeat for the outer border.

Finishing

Refer to Quilting Basics (page 72) to layer, quilt, and bind your quilt.

Tomato Tart

This is called Peasant's Tart in France. Call it what you like—I call it divine. The flavor explodes in your mouth. Please try it. Any tomato will do, from beefsteaks to cherry varieties, but it's best if the tomatoes are not too juicy.* Best of all is if you can obtain local, vine-ripened tomatoes.

*To help prevent a soggy crust, drain sliced tomatoes on paper towels.

- 1 sheet of puff pastry (found in the supermarket frozen foods section, or make your own)
- 4 tablespoons very thick cream (or crème fraîche if available)
- 4 tablespoons Dijon mustard

- 10–12 good-sized tomatoes, sliced (or the equivalent of cherry tomatoes)
- 2–3 cloves of garlic, chopped
- Fresh thyme if available
- Dried thyme and basil
- Sea salt and fresh ground black pepper
- Olive oil

Thaw pastry and roll out on a lightly floured surface. Trim to fit a 10"–12" tart pan with removable bottom (or a quiche pan). Carefully place pastry in pan and crimp edges. Mix together cream and mustard and spread over pastry base. Lightly sprinkle with dried basil, thyme, and chopped garlic. Arrange the sliced tomatoes in an overlapping circular fashion to cover base. Double layer if you have more slices. Season with salt and pepper, drizzle with olive oil, and top with fresh thyme for a great show! Bake in preheated 375°F oven for 40 minutes, or until crust is nicely browned and tomatoes begin to char. Cool slightly before serving.

Gazpacho

Gazpacho is something I had heard about for ages, but, not knowing exactly what it consisted of, I was never tempted to make it. If you feel this way, change your mind right now. Gazpacho, a pungent soup of fresh raw vegetables served cold all over the south and east areas of Spain, is very easy to make and extremely healthy—and it's another Spanish taste explosion! Use a food processor or blender to combine the ingredients.

- 2 pounds ripe tomatoes
- 2 large cucumbers, peeled
- 4 cloves of garlic, peeled
- 2 large red bell peppers, cored and seeded
- 3 tablespoons vinegar
- Small can of tomato sauce
- Scant ½ cup olive oil
- ¼ cup lemon juice
- 2 tablespoons sugar
- ½ teaspoon red pepper flakes
- Sea salt

Roughly chop the vegetables and combine everything well in a large bowl. Process in batches, depending on the size of your food processor or blender. Don't take it all the way to the purée stage—just to this side of it. If the mixture seems too thick (this will depend upon the juice content of the tomatoes), add a bit of cold water. Check and adjust the seasoning to your taste. Chill for several hours while the flavors blend. Each day it gets better. The soup is lovely garnished with finely chopped cucumber and fresh parsley. If you like tomatoes, you will LOVE this soup.

Magenta Magic

Finished quilt size: 65″ × 66″

Made by Roberta Cardew and machine
quilted by Bobbi Lang.

Magenta Magic seemed the perfect
name for this quilt, and furthermore, I
thought this name was original—until
I Googled it, that is. As of this writing, there are 1,060,000 entries for
"Magenta Magic"! You can purchase
everything from a Magenta Magic
screensaver to a Magenta Magic
Pashmina wool and silk shawl from
Kashmir. Evidently I'm not the only
one who thinks magenta is magic!

Color Lesson

This quilt is all about that magical color and is simply raw use of a single hue and shades thereof. It is an elementary but very valuable approach to color: Choose any one of your favorite colors and gather enough shades and variations of that color to make up a quilt. This exercise can be called Theme (main color) and Variations (coordinating fabrics). Theme and Variations is a much used and highly effective practice employed in many art forms, music included. Choose a color, collect its variations, and turn it into a tremendously passionate quilt! I chose magenta, but only because it's magic, anywhere.

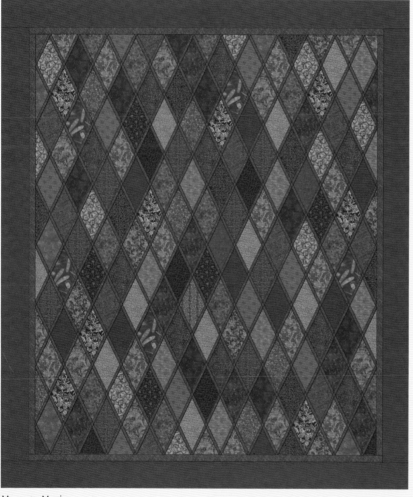

Magenta Magic

Materials

Yardage is based on fabric that measures 40"–42" wide.

- Theme color fabric: ½ yard
- 9 color variations of the theme color: ½ yard of each
- Forest green fabric for the lattice strips and the inner border: 1⅞ yards
- Outer border fabric: 1⅛ yards
- Binding fabric: ⅔ yard
- Backing fabric: 4¼ yards
- Batting: 73" × 74"
- Ruler with marked 60° and 120° angles (optional); or template plastic or paper

Cutting

Cut strips on the crosswise grain, from selvage to selvage.

To cut the diamonds, you can use the template patterns on page 76 or follow the instructions in Cut the Diamonds, Step 1 on page 43.

THEME AND VARIATIONS
FABRICS (10):

From each fabric, cut 3 strips 4″ wide; subcut each into 24 diamonds, as described on page 42.

FOREST GREEN FABRIC:

For the lattice strips, see Cut the Lattice Strips below

For the inner border, cut 6 strips 1½″ wide; join end to end with diagonal seams (see Quilting Basics, page 71).

OUTER BORDER FABRIC:

Cut 7 strips 4½″ wide; join end to end with diagonal seams.

Making the Quilt Top

This quilt has 188 diamonds separated by lattice strips and set in 20 diagonal rows.

CUT THE DIAMONDS

Cut 240 diamonds in all, 24 of each of the 10 colors. This is more than you will need, but a few extra will be good to have so you can mix the colors when placing them. If you are not using the template (page 76), follow the instructions below.

1. With a 4″ strip of the theme fabric lined up on a large cutting board, lay a template or ruler with marked angles at 60° to the baseline as shown. The top angle will be 120°. Use a rotary cutter to cut 1 diamond. Repeat to cut 8 diamonds. Repeat for the other 2 strips to cut a total of 24 diamonds.

Cut the diamonds.

2. Repeat Step 2 with each of the remaining 9 variation colors. Keep the diamonds separated by color.

CUT THE LATTICE STRIPS

1. Cut 21 strips 1″ wide for the lattice strips; subcut these into 4½″ lattice strips, using the same procedure and angles as for cutting the diamonds. Cut a total of 168 strips 1″ × 4½″.

2. Cut an additional 22 strips, 1″ wide. Join them together end to end as needed and subcut into the following lengths:

2 strips 9″ each

2 strips 18″ each

2 strips 27″ each

2 strips 36″ each

2 strips 45″ each

2 strips 54″ each

2 strips 63″ each

5 strips 67″ each

These are the long strips joining the rows of diamonds. They will be a little long at each end, but after the quilt is sewn together, it will be trimmed to exact size.

CREATE THE ROWS

1. Sew 1 lattice strip 4½″ to the top left side of each diamond as shown.

Add lattice strips to diamonds.

2. Sew the diamonds together into 20 rows in a diagonal orientation, positioning them so that a 4½″ green strip lies between every pair of diamonds. Make sure that no two diamonds of the same fabric fall side by side. Arrange them as shown in the assembly diagram to make rows of the following numbers of diamonds:

2 rows of 1 each

2 rows of 3 each

2 rows of 5 each

2 rows of 7 each

2 rows of 9 each

2 rows of 11 each

2 rows of 13 each

6 rows of 15 each

A design wall (see page 11) is extremely useful if not essential for this quilt. (I will admit to laying out quilts on the floor. Although this works, it is not the best route to a good finished product.) I used a design wall to audition the placement of the diamonds for this quilt.

SEW THE ROWS

Refer to the assembly diagram and the assembly chart, page 45.

1. Begin at the bottom left with a single diamond (Row 1). Sew a 9" lattice strip to the top right edge of the Row 1 diamond.

2. Now work toward the top right corner, row by row, alternating diamond rows and lattice strips. Sew a row of 3 diamonds (Row 2) to the 9" lattice strip already in place. Center and sew an 18" lattice strip. Center every row and lattice strip as you go along. As you attach the rows, take special care to line up the cross strips. Press.

The lattice strip will be too long for each row it is first sewn to, but center it; you will use the excess when joining the next row of diamonds. The next diamond row will extend a bit past the strip. Center that row and don't be concerned, because both the excess strip and excess diamonds will be trimmed away later to square up the quilt. This is easier and tidier than fitting numerous fractions of diamonds.

ASSEMBLY CHART

Row	Number of Diamonds	Length of Lattice Strip
1	1	9"
2	3	18"
3	5	27"
4	7	36"
5	9	45"
6	11	54"
7	13	63"
8	15	67"
9	15	67"
10	15	67"
11	15	67"
12	15	67"
13	15	63"
14	13	54"
15	11	45"
16	9	36"
17	7	27"
18	5	18"
19	3	9"
20	1	None

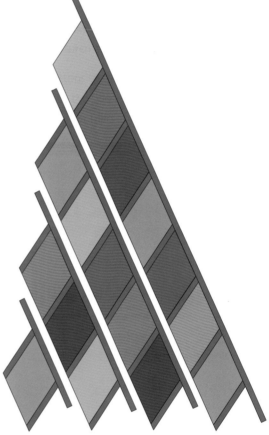

Assembly diagram

TRIM THE EDGES

Using a large cutting mat, long ruler, and rotary cutter, trim off the excess at the edges to square up the quilt top.

ATTACH THE BORDERS

There are 2 squared borders—a narrow inner border and a wider outer border. Refer to Quilting Basics (page 71) to measure and attach the inner border; repeat for the outer border.

FINISHING

Refer to Quilting Basics (page 72) to layer, quilt, and bind your quilt.

Music of the Dawn

Finished quilt size: 58″ × 68″
Finished block size: 10″ × 10″

Made by Roberta Cardew and machine quilted by Bobbi Lang.

Albadas, the name of our village, or *masia*, is surely no accident; in English it translates to *"music of the dawn."* When the sun sinks in the evening behind purple and mauve mountains, it sets your soul aglow; and when it reappears in splendor the next morning, it is with an unparalleled palette.

Our village's lovely name, coupled with the lovely sounds that happen as the earth is awakening—light breezes stirring the leaves of almond and olive trees, birds and small animals moving about—has been the inspiration for this quilt.

Its design is a slight variation of the traditional Log Cabin design. Its success lies entirely upon color, just like the sunrise! It can be made easily from a fabric stash, from fabrics purchased particularly for the quilt, or more probably, from a combination of the two. I definitely used a combination.

Color Lesson

This quilt requires a collection of brilliantly colored fabrics that will be cut into strips to surround a common square center block in Log Cabin fashion.

Choose a fabric you find especially pleasing from which to make all the center blocks (the featured fabric), and coordinate the remaining fabrics—3 or 30—around that primary piece. Your featured fabric may require fussy cutting, depending on its design.

The following advice may sound elementary, but it is a basic principle of quilt designing that you will use over and over again: If you are at a loss regarding where to begin, follow your heart and choose the fabric that speaks loudest to you as the principal fabric. Then choose its "friends" as secondary fabrics. A relaxed attitude is required here. I used 21 colors, but there is nothing magic about that number; just make sure you have a good variety. Choose from your fabric stash and augment with purchased fat quarters. You may want to select the secondary fabrics with a theme in mind— for this quilt, the colors of a beautiful sunrise!

I'm not giving you a lot of specific direction on color choice here. Because this quilt is a simple pattern that is fairly easy to assemble, I thought it would be a good opportunity for you to practice designing by selecting your colors and placing them in the quilt as you see fit. Have fun!

Charms of Albadas

As I've mentioned, our home is a small masia, or village, located in the mountains that hug the Mediterranean Sea up and down the eastern coast of Spain. The area is infused with a captivating charm, and the lifestyle is light years away from the bustle of seaside resorts located less than an hour's drive away.

In this neighborhood, shepherds still meander with their sheep among ancient and gnarled olive trees; fresh produce is sold at weekly open-air markets; and the male population, young and old, chase bulls through the streets during certain fiestas and designated times of the year.

There are very few sewing machines in this rural area. In fact, the neighbors who bring their mending and altering to me assure me that mine is the only sewing machine in all of Castellón Province! This is a great exaggeration, but I do my best to appear appropriately impressed by the compliment, and I graciously accept the opportunity to become part of the community.

Music of the Dawn

Materials

Yardage is based on fabric that measures 40"–42" wide.

- Featured fabric: 1 yard for the center squares*
- Secondary fabrics, 15–21 different fabrics for the block strips (see Color Lesson, page 47): 4–4½ yards total
- Inner border fabric: ½ yard
- Outer border fabric: 1 yard
- Backing fabric: 3⅞ yards
- Binding: ⅝ yard
- Batting: 66" × 75"

If you choose a fabric that must be fussy cut, you will need 1½–2 yards.

Cutting

FEATURED FABRIC:

Cut 30 squares 6" × 6".

SECONDARY FABRICS:

See Cut the Strips, below.

INNER BORDER FABRIC:

Cut 7 strips 1½" × width of the fabric.

OUTER BORDER FABRIC:

Cut 7 strips 3½" × width of the fabric.

Making the Quilt Top

This quilt has 30 blocks. Each has the same center fabric, but the color combinations of the surrounding strips will be different for each block.

CUT THE STRIPS

You will need a total of 360 "log" pieces to complete the blocks. The pieces are labeled A through F. All the A's for each block are the same fabric and width, all B's are the same, and so forth. They are subnumbered 1 and 2 for ease of assembly.

From each of the 15–21 fabrics, cut the strips in the following widths:

    1" wide (A's and B's)

    1½" wide (C's and D's)

    1¼" wide (E's and F's)

ASSEMBLE THE BLOCKS

1. Begin with a 6" square block of the featured fabric. Sew an A1 strip to the left side of the block. Proceed counterclockwise to attach strip A2 (same color, same width as A1) to the bottom of the block. Press as you go along.

2. Choose a new color for B1 and B2. Continuing counterclockwise around the center square, attach as you did A1 and A2.

3. Repeat this process with strips C through F, as shown below. Press.

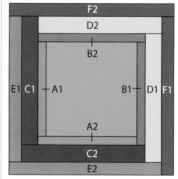

Sew strips around block center.

4. Repeat to construct 30 blocks with the same center and greatly varying surrounding strips.

SEW THE ROWS

Blocks are sewn together without the use of sashing.

1. Arrange the blocks on a design wall or any flat surface, taking care not to place the same colors side by side. It is okay to rotate blocks and change their orientation to achieve this. Refer to the quilt on page 46.

2. Sew together 5 blocks to form a row. Repeat to make 6 rows. Press.

3. Sew together the 6 rows. Press.

ATTACH THE BORDERS

There are 2 squared borders—a narrow inner border and a wider outer border. Refer to Quilting Basics (page 71) to measure and attach the inner border; repeat for the outer border.

Finishing

Refer to Quilting Basics (page 72) to layer, quilt, and bind your quilt.

Don't worry about cutting the strips into lengths to fit. If you use fabrics from your stash, the strips will probably be varying lengths. This is fine, as long as the strips are the correct width. When you sew them into the block, you can simply position an end where it should begin and stitch the seam until you reach the end of the piece to which you are attaching the strip. At this point, cut off the excess length of strip and return it to the table. Remember that for each block, you will need to cut pairs of the log pieces from the same fabric.

When cutting, it is good to overproduce, so that you have plenty of options as you assemble. You may want to cut some of the strips at the beginning, and then cut more as you go along. You will know better what colors you prefer once you've gotten into the project.

You will have much more control over the placement of color than if you tried to cut all 360 pieces to exact fit at the onset.

TIP

The quilt will go together more easily if you spend a little time up front organizing the strips. It is a good idea to have an empty tabletop or hanging rack so the strips can be organized by color fabric and by width. Keep the three widths of the same color in their own group.

As you sew the strips for each block, you'll be able to easily see and select which fabric to sew on next.

Through the *Music Room Window*

Finished size: 41″ × 50″
Finished block size: 3″ × 6″

Made by Roberta Cardew and machine quilted by Pam Shaw.

Spain is a mysterious and romantic place, and where we live is no exception. A mountain track leads up to the old stone and terra cotta–tiled house perched on the edge of a precipice that descends 200 feet to a dry riverbed, where there are fossils and other magical things. In the house there are many fairy-tale rooms through which to wander, but the most enchanting is the music room.

In addition to three pianos and hundreds of dusty, first-edition and out-of-print books that came to us from my husband's ancestors, the music room has a magnificent window. It is so high on the wall that one needs a ladder in order to close its shutters. We seldom do. There are ornate bars which form a homogeneous grid. Looking through them, you see marvelous things. Although everyone knows there are no songbirds in this area, I saw them, and they were singing among the roses. I listened and thought about quilts. I concluded that through the music room window, there can be anything you want there to be!

For the featured fabric in this quilt, choose a distinctive pattern. Since you are using only one fabric, it needs to be something that truly speaks to you, and something that you could imagine seeing through a window. And not just

Color Lesson

I consider this quilt the most romantic of the collection, partly because of the deep, passionate scarlet of the roses and the striking black of the "window bars"—both strong colors. Matching intensity of color in a quilt is very important.

Having used spectacular color, I wanted to feature it to maximum advantage. There is a pottery-decorating technique called banding, which means to paint a narrow stripe around the edge of a vessel. In a quilt, this technique translates into using a very narrow strip along each side of the quilt to pull a desired color out from the quilt—in this case, the scarlet of the roses. This strip can be considered part of the border, which itself should inject additional life into the quilt. Borders should be used to capture the life of the quilt and extend it beyond the edges, not to act as a fence. Of course, proportion needs to be considered, and since this quilt is a rather small wallhanging, the strips need to be very narrow, whereas in a larger quilt they could be wider.

Another excellent color technique is echoing. The color of the narrow strips is repeated or echoed in the binding. The chosen color jumps from the quilt to the strips, then takes another leap to the binding, thus expanding the quilt.

any window—perhaps a window in a tower of a castle in Spain! I used a fabric with a birds and roses theme.

This quilt relies on repetition to emphasize its central feature, the "window" fabric. The birds and flowers in the featured fabric make such a magnificent statement on their own that they need no competition, only repetition. Using another print would fight with the main one and deaden the quilt. Repetition is well known to quilters and usually applies to the repetition of shapes, also used in this quilt. There is but one printed fabric and one general shape of pieces. All the better for an eye-catching effect is a simplicity which is repeated over and over again!

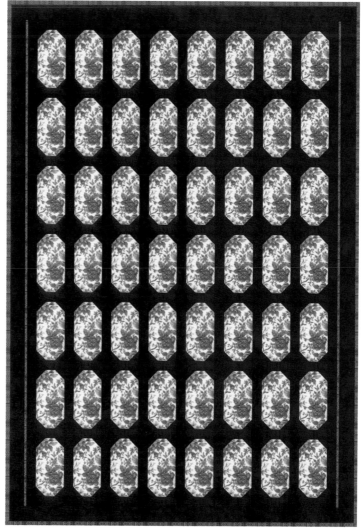

Through the Music Room Window

Materials

Yardage is based on fabrics that measure 40″–42″ wide.

- Featured fabric (Fabric A): 1⅜ yards for the windowpanes
- Black solid fabric (Fabric B): 1½ yards for window bars and borders
- Solid fabric keyed to featured fabric (Fabric C): 2⅛ yards total (⅛ yard for narrow border strips, ⅜ yard for binding, and 1⅝ yards for backing)*
- Batting: 49″ × 58″
- Fabric marker with a fine point and disappearing ink

*You may choose a different fabric for binding and backing if you wish, but I prefer that the binding, at least, match the narrow strips.

My all-time favorite fabric marker is the Sewline Fabric Pencil. The lines are clean, clear, precise, and easily removed with moisture. It is possible to draw a very thin line that stays in place until you decide to dampen it.

Cutting

Cut strips on the crosswise grain, from selvage to selvage.

FABRIC A:

For the windowpanes, cut 6 strips 6½″ wide; subcut into 56 rectangles 3½″ × 6½″.

FABRIC B:

Cut 18 strips 1″ wide. Using diagonal seams, sew together end to end as needed and cut into 2 strips 48″ long, 8 strips 30″ long, and 49 strips 6½″ long for the window bars and side strips (see Quilting Basics, page 71).

Cut 9 strips 1½″ wide; subcut into 224 squares 1½″ × 1½″ for the windowpane corners.

Cut 5 strips 2½″ wide; join end to end using diagonal seams for borders.

FABRIC C:

Cut 3 strips ¾″ wide, and sew together end to end with diagonal seams (see Quilting Basics, page 71). Cut into 2 strips 48″ long for the side strips.

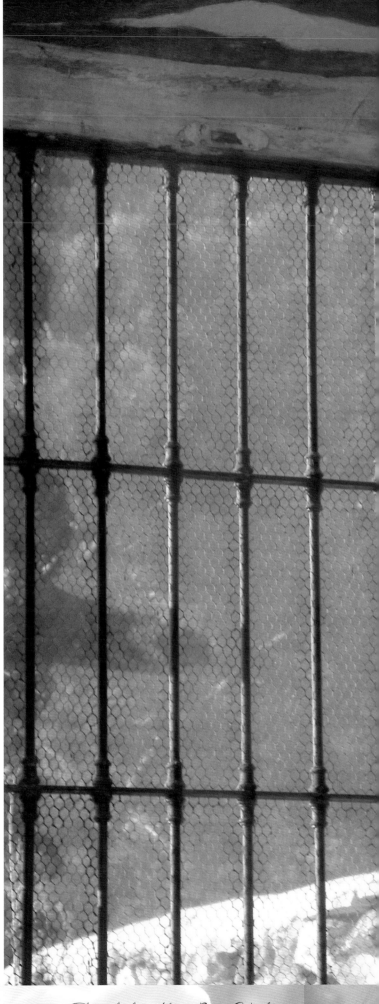

Making the Quilt Top

This quilt has 56 windowpane blocks.

MAKE THE BLOCKS

1. Begin with the 2½" squares of Fabric B. With a fabric marking pen or pencil, carefully draw a diagonal stitching guideline across each square from corner to corner. Refer to the Tips on page 27 for hints for marking and sewing accurately.

2. Position 1 square at each corner of a Fabric A rectangle, with the drawn lines facing up, and stitch along the lines.

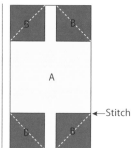

Stitch block corners.

3. Repeat to make 56 blocks.

4. Fold back the inner corners of the squares toward the outside opposite corners and press. This creates the triangle needed at each corner of the windowpane. Use spray sizing on the corners as you press, and do not trim the excess fabric at the backs of the triangles. There will be 3 layers of fabric, but this lends wonderful stability to the corners.

SEW THE ROWS

Each row has 8 windowpane blocks 6½" × 3½", and 7 Fabric B strips 6½" × 1".

1. Beginning with a windowpane block, sew together alternating blocks and Fabric B strips to make a row. End with a windowpane block. Repeat to make a total of 7 rows. Press.

Row of blocks and strips

2. Sew a 1" × 30" Fabric B strip to the top edge of the top row. Sew another strip to the bottom edge and add the second row. Continue alternating strips and blocks to join all 7 rows, ending with a Fabric B strip at the bottom. Take care to align the black vertical strips as you work down the quilt. Trim to even up the side edges. Press.

Assembly diagram

ADD THE SIDE STRIPS

1. Sew a Fabric B 48"-long strip to each side of the quilt. These will be a bit long but will be trimmed later when you square the corners.

2. Sew a Fabric C 48"-long strip to each outer side edge of the quilt. These will be too long but will be trimmed when you square the corners.

3. Using a mat, ruler, and rotary cutter, square up the corners of the quilt.

ATTACH THE BORDERS

Refer to Quilting Basics (page 71) to attach the borders.

Finishing

Use the remaining 2 yards of Fabric C or fabrics of your choice for the backing and binding. Refer to Quilting Basics (page 72) to layer, quilt, and bind the quilt.

Grapes and Green Olives

Finished quilt size: 57″ × 59″

Made by Roberta Cardew and machine quilted by Bobbi Lang.

If you intentionally blur your vision just a bit, it will be obvious that this quilt is a spatter of grapes and green olives with a splash of golden sunshine to make them grow! What could be more quintessentially Spanish than grapes and green olives?

There is a thick vine, gnarled and disfigured with age, that snakes its way across the south side of the house and produces the most exquisite red-purple grapes with neither involvement nor encouragement from us. It grows past the kitchen window. So as I cook, stir, chop, and mash, I can watch the tiny, hard, green globes swell and turn into glorious purple grapes.

In addition to picking grapes from the vine, we actually managed to grow olives and produce our own olive oil (the story on the right). To commemorate that event, *Grapes and Green Olives* was made. It consists of 7 columns of tricolor and striped blocks, each 6″-wide, finished size, separated by 6 vertical sashes of coordinating fabric 2″-wide, finished size. The same coordinating fabric is used to frame the quilt in a 1¼″ border.

Color Lesson

I made this quilt because I fell in love with the colors of the fabrics and because they so much reminded me of the grapes that grow outside our windows and the olive trees all around. Some of the fabric had a swirling pattern, just like grape vines. But mostly, the fabrics were all just right—the solids, prints, stripes—and the colors were of the same subtlety achieving the desired effect of seeming to flow into each other. This seldom happens in my experience, but when it does, it becomes an object of inspiration. Be listening and watching, because from time to time, for no obvious reason, fabric will speak to you, begging you to take it home...just like that puppy in the pet shop window.

English Potter Goes Native

I think being able to have your own olive oil is more or less a miracle! Most of the olives growing near our house are wild, just as the thyme, rosemary, and fennel are. When we bought an adjacent property, my husband, Seth, was delighted to discover that we had purchased an ancient, neglected, totally abandoned grove of olive trees in the deal. More than delighted, Seth was ecstatic. The English potter became the Spanish farmer and went straight to work tending and pruning. Olives grow best on horizontal branches, so those branches reaching too energetically toward the sun were eliminated. The ground was fertilized by local donkeys (the proper thing for olive trees, I understand).

To know when olives are ready to pick, one needs only watch what the neighbors are doing. In this rural area, every farmer has a few olive trees. Since olive trees live almost forever, trees stay in families for generations.

When harvest time arrived, Seth picked his olives with great ceremony, one by one, and carefully packed them into crates. Off they went to the local *co-operativa* to be magically pressed into oil—extra virgin and all that. Finally, word came that the oil was ready—the payoff for months of active effort (and superb siestas in the shade of all those horizontal branches). Seth was off to collect his liquid gold.

That first year's harvest gave us beautiful oil of a divine translucent green with a taste Bertolli could never rival. Ah, the joy of it! We hardly noticed that all that labor had produced barely a gallon of oil. Never mind; it was, after all, a labor of love.

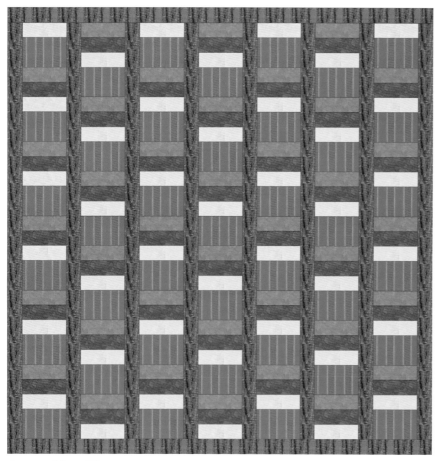

Grapes and Green Olives

Vineyard near Albadas

Materials

Yardage is based on fabric that measures 40" wide.

- Gray-green fabric (Fabric A): ⅔ yard

- Purple fabric (Fabric B): ⅔ yard

- Gold/mustard fabric (Fabric C): 4⅞ yards total (⅔ yard for blocks and 4¼ yards for backing and binding)*

- Coordinating striped fabric (Fabric D): 1 yard

- Coordinating marbled fabric for the sashing and borders (Fabric E): 1⅛ yards

- Batting: 65" × 67"

If you wish, you can choose a fabric different from the gold/mustard for the backing and binding; you will need 4¼ yards.

Cutting

Cut strips on the crosswise grain, from selvage to selvage.

FABRIC A:

For the quilt blocks, cut 7 strips 2½"; subcut into 38 rectangles 6½" × 2½".

FABRIC B:

Cut 7 strips 2½"; subcut into 38 rectangles 6½" × 2½".

FABRIC C:

Cut 7 strips 2½"; subcut into 42 rectangles 6½" × 2½". The remaining fabric will be used for backing and binding.

FABRIC D:

Cut 39 blocks 6½" × 4½".

FABRIC E:

Cut 9 strips 2½" for the sashing, and join together end to end as needed, using diagonal seams (see Quilting Basics, page 71). Cut into 6 strips 56½" long for sashing.

Cut 6 strips 1¾" for the borders. Join together end to end as needed, using diagonal seams.

Making the Quilt Top

This quilt has 38 tricolor blocks.

MAKE THE BLOCKS

1. Sew together a Fabric A, a Fabric B, and a Fabric C rectangle along the 6½" sides, with Fabric B in the center, to make a 6½" × 6½" block. Press.

Block layout

2. Repeat to make a total of 38 tricolor blocks; press. There will be 4 remaining rectangles of Fabric C for use in assembling the columns.

ASSEMBLE THE COLUMNS

There are 2 patterns of construction for the columns of blocks: Pattern 1 and Pattern 2.

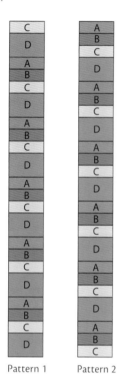

Pattern 1   Pattern 2

Pattern 1

1. Begin at the top of the column with a single rectangle of Fabric C and attach a block of Fabric D. Then add a tricolor block with the Fabric A strip at the top.

2. Using 5 tricolor blocks and 6 blocks of Fabric D, continue joining blocks in an alternating fashion, ending with a block of Fabric D as shown in the Column Pattern 1 diagram above. Construct a total of 4 columns of Pattern 1. Press.

Pattern 2

1. Begin at the top of the column using a tricolor block with the Fabric A strip at the top. Attach a block of Fabric D.

2. Using 6 tricolor blocks and 5 Fabric D blocks, join blocks together in an alternating fashion, ending with a tricolor block as shown in the Column Pattern 2 diagram to the left. Construct a total of 3 columns of Pattern 2. Press.

ASSEMBLE THE COLUMNS

Beginning with a Pattern 1 column at the left, sew a 2½"-wide sashing strip to the right long edge. Sew a Pattern 2 column to the right edge of the sashing strip. Continue alternating columns and sashing strips across the quilt, ending with a Pattern 1 column. Press.

Pattern 1   Pattern 2   Pattern 1   Pattern 2   Pattern 1   Pattern 2   Pattern 1

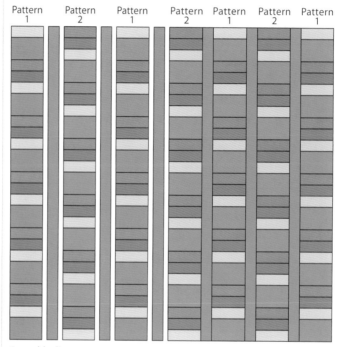

Assembly diagram

ATTACH THE BORDER

Refer to Quilting Basics (page 71) to attach the borders.

Finishing

Use the remainder of Fabric C, or a fabric of your choice, for the backing and binding. Refer to Quilting Basics (page 72) to layer, quilt, and bind the quilt.

Marinated Olives

This is a simple, attractive, and delicious treatment for olives—anywhere! It is best when an assortment of olives is used. I use our little black ones, which have been preserved in brine. The others are purchased from the olive vendor at the weekly market in Val d'Alba. In most American supermarkets, a great variety of olives are available. Black olives, unstuffed green olives, and Kalamata olives make a good mixture.

Drain off brine from olives and rinse well. When dried, tip into a bowl and add herbs:

- 1 bay leaf, fresh or dried
- Dried thyme
- Dried oregano
- Red pepper flakes
- Thinly sliced fresh garlic
- Olive oil

Gently mix and add olive oil to cover olives. Cover and let marinate two days if you can wait. The flavors mix best at room temperature and improve with age. Before serving, add a few slices of fresh lemon.

The Oleander Bush

Finished quilt size: 68″ × 68″
Finished block size: 13″ × 13″

Made by Roberta Cardew and machine quilted by Bobbi Lang.

This hardy bush, actually a large shrub, grows profusely in Spain and in most areas around the Mediterranean Sea—even in our dry, stony riverbed! If plants have spirits, I would say the spirit of the oleander is sublimely courageous. Summer after summer, this evergreen bursts forth into an abundance of flowers—most often in shades of brilliant pinks—and asks nothing in return. It springs from beds of stone and gravel, seemingly requiring neither soil nor water. The heat of summer does not affect its performance, nor do the harsh winters in these coastal mountain ranges. It is often used in mass plantings along main motorways, and these flowers object not at all to the unbearable heat and vehicle fumes. They do so brighten a journey.

I realize that the oleander grows in many other places as well, but in Spain was my first true exposure to this wonderful plant. I cannot sing its praises highly enough, and its colors are formidable. Of course, this quilt is in honor of the oleander bush.

Color Lesson

The colors of our oleanders are echoed in the principal part of this quilt. I chose two shades of rose-colored batiks for two reasons: The colors of batiks have a certain intensity that is pleasing, plus the slight suggestion of a pattern, which lends interest and movement. All of this is important when using a large amount of only one or two fabrics. There is certainly nothing wrong with traditional solids per se, but when used over a large area, they can tend to go a bit flat, deflated. As quilters, we need to avail ourselves of every opportunity to bring life and movement into our creations—batiks work for me. This is a simple, straightforward patchwork quilt designed to show off a chosen color. I chose two rose colors of similar intensities but dissimilar shades.

The Oleander Bush

The Oleander Bush

Materials

Yardage is based on fabric that measures 40" wide.

- Fabric in 2 shades of rose (Fabrics X and Y): 1½ yards of each for the blocks

- Fabrics in 4 coordinating pink prints (Fabrics A, B, C, and D): ⅓ yard of each for the short block strips

- Fabrics in 4 coordinating green prints (Fabrics E, F, G, and H): ½ yard of each print for the longer block strips

- Border fabric: ½ yard

- Backing and binding fabric: 4⅞ yards

- Batting: 76" × 76"

Cutting

Cut strips on the crosswise grain, from selvage to selvage.

FABRICS X AND Y:

From each fabric, cut 8 strips 5½" wide; subcut into 50 squares 5½" × 5½".

FABRICS A, B, C, AND D:

From each fabric, cut 4 strips 2" wide; subcut into 25 strips 2" × 5½".

FABRICS E, F, G, AND H:

From each fabric, cut 5 strips 2" wide; subcut into 25 strips 2" × 7" of each.

BORDER FABRIC:

Cut into 7 strips 2" wide; join together end to end using diagonal seams (see Quilting Basics, page 71).

Making the Quilt Top

MAKE THE BLOCKS

This quilt has 25 blocks. Each block is made up of 4 square block sections, each of which combines a Fabric X or Y square with short and long strips.

Assemble the block sections

1. Sew a Fabric A strip to one side of a Fabric X square. Turn the square and sew a Fabric E strip to the adjoining side. Repeat to make a total of 25 X/A/E squares. Press.

2. Using 1 of the remaining 25 blocks of Fabric X, sew a strip of Fabric B to one side. Turn the square and sew a Fabric F strip to the adjoining side. Repeat to make a total of 25 X/B/F squares. Press.

3. Sew a Fabric C strip to one side of a Fabric Y square. Turn the square and sew a Fabric G strip to the adjoining side. Repeat to make a total of 25 Y/C/G squares. Press.

4. Using 1 of the remaining 25 blocks of Fabric Y, sew a strip of Fabric D to one side, turn the square, and sew a Fabric H strip to adjoining side. Repeat to make a total of 25 Y/D/H squares. Press.

5. You now have 100 square block sections, 7″ × 7″, in 4 different color combinations. Keep them separate for ease in further assembly.

Assemble the blocks

1. Select a block section from each of the 4 color combinations, and sew them together with the strips toward the center as shown. Press.

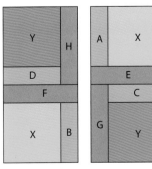

Block assembly

2. You now have 25 identical blocks 13½″ × 13½″.

SEW THE ROWS

1. As you sew the blocks together into rows, take care to keep them in the same orientation. Sew 5 blocks together, side by side, to form a row. Repeat until you have 5 rows of blocks all in the same orientation. Press.

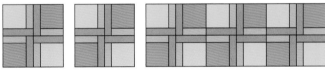

Sew the blocks into rows.

2. Join the 5 rows of 5 blocks each. Press.

ATTACH THE BORDER

Refer to Quilting Basics (page 71), to attach the borders.

Finishing

Refer to Quilting Basics (page 72) to layer, quilt, and bind the quilt.

Seasons of Sunsets

Finished size: 70″ × 70″
Finished large block size: 20″ × 20″

Made by Roberta Cardew and machine quilted by Marcella Pickett of Crooked Creek Quilts.

Most people in these small Spanish mountain communities are perfectly in step with the seasons of life. There is no questioning who they are, no searching for an identity. Each day with its unique, yet timeless, activities is entered into with perfect familiarity, rehearsed from time eternal. The clock at the local restaurant has been at the same time for many years, and it would be disturbing if it should ever begin to run. Here, you can always, always count on paella on Wednesday!

It is a comfortable feeling to allow oneself to blend into what is happening. In the meantime, though, the sun continues its evening performance of awesome repetition. At sunset, the sun is momentarily suspended in a world where life itself seems at times a surreal sensation. It is a sensation that happens quite often at the seaside as well. The waves come in, flow out, and advance again on top of each other in a perfect rhythm that has no beginning and no end.

This quilt is meant as a tribute to the glorious and undying sunsets of Albadas that set the sky on fire.

Color Lesson

The colors of the fabrics used in this quilt are intense, as they must be to represent a sunset. The quilt contains fifteen different fabrics in vibrant prints and batiks. Take care that the twelve prints for the circles flow well together in color as well as in form.

This is not at all a difficult quilt to make. The entire quilt is composed using only three pattern pieces, two different sizes of wedges and a setting piece. When I was assembling it at the shop, a few customers, kindly interested in what's happening in my corner, fessed up that they were intimidated by circles. My comment on that is if you can handle triangles, circles are a piece of cake! So carry on, my friends, into a season of sunsets rich in color.

Seasons of Sunsets

Materials

Yardage is based on fabric that measures 40″ wide.

- 12 different and intensely colored print fabrics: ½ yard each for the small and large circles
- Light orange batik: 1 yard for the circle setting pieces
- Dark orange batik: 1 yard for the circle setting pieces
- Purple batik: 2 yards for the circle setting pieces and 1¾ yards for the border and binding
- Backing fabric: 4½ yards
- Batting: 78″ × 78″
- Template plastic or paper

 As mentioned earlier, this is not a difficult quilt to make, but its successful assembly depends absolutely on accurately cut pieces and strict use of ¼″ seams.

Cutting

Patterns are on pages 77–78. Use template plastic or paper to trace and cut out template patterns A, B, and C.

12 PRINT FABRICS:

Use pattern piece A to cut 144 large wedges and pattern piece B to cut 108 small wedges, all of various prints.

LIGHT ORANGE FABRIC:

Use pattern piece C to cut 8 setting pieces.

DARK ORANGE FABRIC:

Use pattern piece C to cut 8 setting pieces.

PURPLE FABRIC:

Use pattern piece C to cut 20 setting pieces.

BORDER FABRIC:

Cut 8 strips 5½″ × width of the fabric. Join end to end using diagonal seams (see Quilting Basics, page 71). Reserve the remaining fabric to use as binding.

Making the Quilt Top

 Since almost none of the cut edges in this quilt are on the straight grain of the fabric, use spray sizing as you go. It helps to stabilize the pieces.

The quilt is assembled in 3 parts: you will make 36 small blocks, join them together in fours to make 9 large blocks, and finally join these to create the 9-block quilt top.

MAKE THE SMALL BLOCKS

Construct 36 small blocks. Each block requires 4 A pieces, 3 B pieces, and 1 C piece.

1. Sew together 4 A pieces in pie fashion. First sew 2 pieces together, and then sew the other 2 on either end of the fan to make the large wedge. Press, using spray starch.
2. Sew together 3 of piece B as you did the A pieces to make the small wedge. Press.
3. Attach the large wedge to the widest arc of piece C. (No snipping of curves on piece C is required.) To find the center of the larger arc, fold piece C in half and press. Match the center of the curved edge of the large wedge to the center of C, and pin. Pin also at the beginning and at the end. Carefully stitch, using a ¼″ seam, rounding the curve slowly. The 2 pieces will "melt" together. Try not to stretch either fabric. (If the pieces have been accurately cut and pressed using spray sizing, stretching should not be necessary, although it's always a temptation to do so!)
4. Sew the small wedge to the smaller arc on C, using the same method. Press.

5. Repeat Steps 1 through 4 to make a total of 36 small blocks: 8 with orange piece C, 8 with light orange, and 20 with purple. Square up the blocks to measure 10½″ × 10½″.

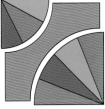 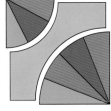 

Make 8. Make 8. Make 20.

Small block

MAKE THE LARGE BLOCKS

Each large block requires 4 small blocks. When joining the 4 small blocks, use blocks with the same color piece C, finishing with the large circle of wedges in the center.

1. Sew 2 small blocks together, joining and matching the large wedges.

2. Repeat Step 1 using 2 more small blocks with the same color of piece C.

3. Sew the 2 pairs of blocks together to form a "sun" in the middle.

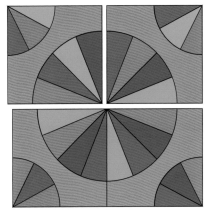

Large block

4. Repeat to make a total of 2 large blocks using orange batik as piece C, 2 blocks using light orange, and 5 blocks using purple. Square up the blocks to measure 20½″ × 20½″. Press.

ASSEMBLE THE BLOCKS

Sew together the 9 blocks in 3 rows of 3 blocks each. Match the seams of the small circles formed at the corners. See the full quilt layout (page 67) for color placement.

ATTACH THE BORDER

Refer to Quilting Basics (page 71) to attach the borders.

Finishing

Refer to Quilting Basics (page 72) to layer, quilt, and bind the quilt. Use the remaining rich purple fabric for binding.

Spanish Vegetable Pie

This is a rich and scrumptious quiche sort of pie that uses sliced potatoes for the crust, to reflect the Spanish love of potatoes (*papas*). It's a wonderful recipe that spirals around and around and manifesting itself in the rampant colors of a proper sunset. It is superb!

- 2–3 pounds of red potatoes
- 8 ounces soft cream cheese
- 3 eggs, beaten
- ½ cup thick cream or half and half
- ¾ cup grated sharp cheddar cheese
- 6–8 green onions, chopped
- 1 large red bell pepper
- Large bunch of fresh spinach or other garden green, such as chard
- 2 teaspoons Dijon mustard
- Dash of nutmeg
- Olive oil
- Sea salt and fresh ground black pepper

Scrub the potatoes but leave the peel intact. Thinly slice them; a mandolin works very well for this job. Arrange potato slices concentrically, beginning in the center of the dish. Generously season the arranged potatoes with salt and pepper and drizzle with olive oil. I have used a deep 10″ pie dish with a generous lip. But I realize that not everyone is married to a potter, so if you don't have this size pie dish, improvise with what you have. It will taste just as good.

Wash and drain the spinach or greens. Wilt in a skillet with a bit of olive oil. Let as much moisture evaporate as you can without burning the greens. Cool slightly.

In a large bowl, combine the softened cream cheese, eggs, cream, ½ cup of the grated cheddar, chopped green onions, nutmeg, and mustard. Mix well. Add the cooled spinach and mix again. Carefully pour over the sliced potatoes, trying not to disarrange them.

Cut the red pepper in half, vertically, and then slice into vertical strips. Lay them on top of the pie in a circular fashion. Carefully drizzle a bit more olive oil over the potatoes that are showing around the edge of the pie. It will allow them to turn a wonderful golden color during baking.

Bake in a preheated 375°F oven for approximately 40 minutes. Test for doneness as you would a cake, by inserting a knife into the center of the pie. About halfway through baking, sprinkle the remaining ¼ cup of grated cheddar on top. It will brown beautifully; and indeed, beautiful it is!

Quiltmaking Basics: How to Finish Your Quilt

General Guidelines

SEAM ALLOWANCES

A ¼" seam allowance is used for most projects. It's a good idea to do a test seam before you begin sewing to check that your ¼" is accurate. Accuracy is the key to successful piecing.

There is no need to backstitch. Seamlines will be crossed by another seam, which will anchor them.

PRESSING

In general, press seams toward the darker fabric. Press lightly in an up-and-down motion. Avoid using a very hot iron or over-ironing, which can distort shapes and blocks. Be especially careful when pressing bias edges because they stretch easily. This is when you really need spray sizing.

Joining Strips with Diagonal Seams

Place the strips right sides together at a 90° angle as shown. Sew from corner to corner, and trim the seam allowance to ¼". Press the seams open.

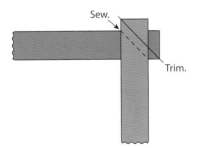

Sew from corner to corner.

Completed diagonal seam

Borders

When border strips are cut on the crosswise grain, piece the strips together to achieve the needed lengths.

SQUARED BORDERS

In most cases the side borders are sewn on first. When you have finished the quilt top, measure it through the center vertically. This will be the length to cut the side borders. Place pins at the centers of all 4 sides of the quilt top, as well as in the center of each side border strip. Pin the side borders to the quilt top first, matching the center pins. Using a ¼" seam allowance, sew the borders to the quilt top and press toward the border.

Measure horizontally across the center of the quilt top, including the side borders. This will be the length to cut the top and bottom borders. Repeat pinning, sewing, and pressing.

Backing

Plan on making the backing a minimum of 8" longer and wider than the quilt top. Piece, if necessary. Trim the selvages before you piece to the desired size.

Batting

The type of batting to use is a personal decision; consult your local quilt shop. Cut batting approximately 8" longer and wider than your quilt top. Note that your batting choice will affect how much quilting is necessary for the quilt. Check the manufacturer's instructions to see how far apart the quilting lines can be.

Layering

Spread the backing wrong side up and tape the edges down with masking tape. (If you are working on carpet, you can use T-pins to secure the backing to the carpet.) Center the batting on top, smoothing out any folds. Place the quilt top right side up on top of the batting and backing, making sure it is centered.

Basting

Basting keeps the quilt "sandwich" layers from shifting while you are quilting.

If you plan to machine quilt, pin baste the quilt layers together with safety pins placed a minimum of 3"–4" apart. Begin basting in the center and move toward the edges, first in vertical rows, then in horizontal rows. Try not to pin directly on the intended quilting lines.

If you plan to hand quilt, baste the layers together with thread using a long needle and light-colored thread. Knot one end of the thread. Using stitches approximately the length of the needle, begin in the center and move out toward the edges in vertical and horizontal rows approximately 4" apart. Add 2 diagonal rows of basting.

Quilting

Quilting, whether by hand or machine, enhances the pieced or appliquéd design of the quilt. You may choose to quilt in-the-ditch, echo the pieced or appliqué motifs, use patterns from quilting design books and stencils, or do your own free-motion quilting. Remember to check your batting manufacturer's recommendations for how close the quilting lines must be.

Binding

Trim excess batting and backing from the quilt evenly with the edges of the quilt top.

DOUBLE-FOLD STRAIGHT-GRAIN BINDING

If you want a ¼" finished binding, cut the binding strips 2" wide and piece them together with diagonal seams to make a continuous binding strip (refer to Joining Strips with Diagonal Seams, page 71).

Press the entire strip in half lengthwise with wrong sides together. With raw edges even, pin the binding to the front edge of the quilt a few inches away from the corner, and leave the first few inches of the binding unattached. Start sewing, using a ¼" seam allowance.

Stop ¼" away from the first corner (see Step 1), and then backstitch one stitch. Lift the presser foot and needle. Rotate the quilt one-quarter turn. Fold the binding at a right angle so it extends straight above the quilt and the fold forms a 45° angle in the corner (see Step 2). Then bring the binding strip down even with the edge of the quilt (see Step 3). Begin sewing at the folded edge. Repeat in the same manner at all corners.

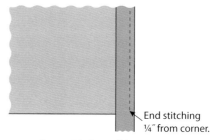

Step 1. Stitch to ¼" from corner.

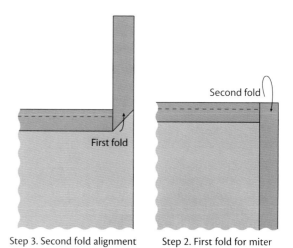

Step 3. Second fold alignment   Step 2. First fold for miter

Continue stitching until you are back near the beginning of the binding strip. See Finishing the Binding Ends for tips on finishing and hiding the raw edges of the ends of the binding.

FINISHING THE BINDING ENDS

Method 1:

After stitching around the quilt, fold under the beginning tail of the binding strip ¼" so that the raw edge will be inside the binding after it is turned to the backside of the quilt. Place the end tail of the binding strip over the beginning folded end.

Continue to attach the binding and stitch slightly beyond the starting stitches. Trim the excess binding. Fold the binding over the raw edges to the quilt back and hand stitch, mitering the corners.

Method 2:

(See our blog entry at http://www.ctpubblog.com/2009/03/23/quilting-tips-completing-a-binding-with-an-invisible-seam/.)

Fold the ending tail of the binding back on itself where it meets the beginning binding tail. From the fold, measure and mark the cut width of your binding strip. Cut the ending binding tail to this measurement. For example, if your binding is cut 2⅛" wide, measure from the fold on the ending tail of the binding 2⅛" and cut the binding tail to this length.

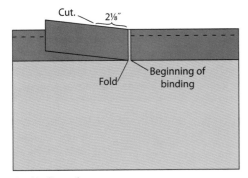

Cut binding tail.

Open both tails. Place 1 tail on top of the other tail at right angles, right sides together. Mark a diagonal line from corner to corner and stitch on the line. Check that you've done it correctly and that the binding fits the quilt, and then trim the seam allowance to ¼". Press open.

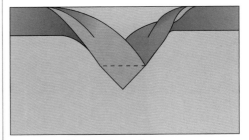

Stitch ends of binding diagonally.

Refold the binding and stitch this binding section in place on the quilt. Fold the binding over the raw edges to the quilt back and hand stitch.

Template Patterns

In Spanish Fields

Searching for Sailboats

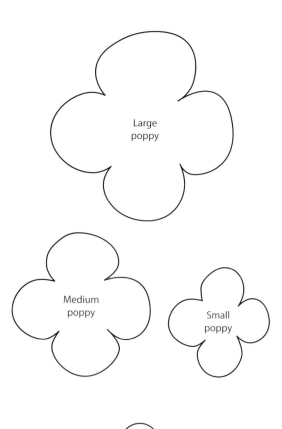

Large
poppy

Medium
poppy

Small
poppy

Center for
large and medium
poppies

Center for
small poppy

Cut approximately 200 poppies of varying sizes and colors.

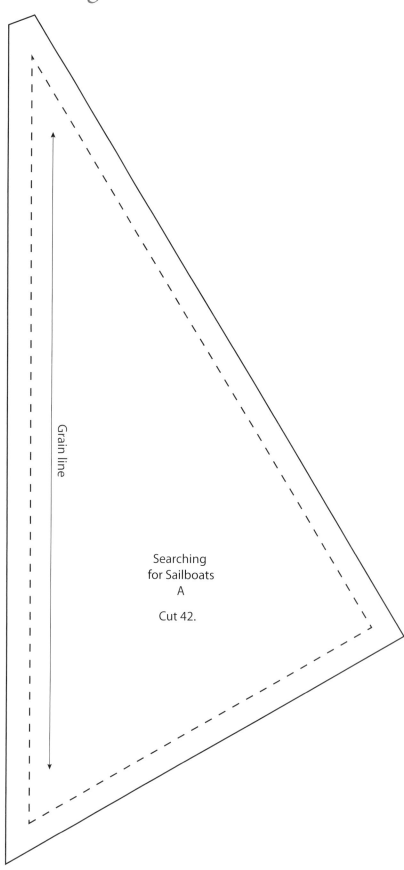

Grain line

Searching
for Sailboats
A

Cut 42.

From Spain with Love

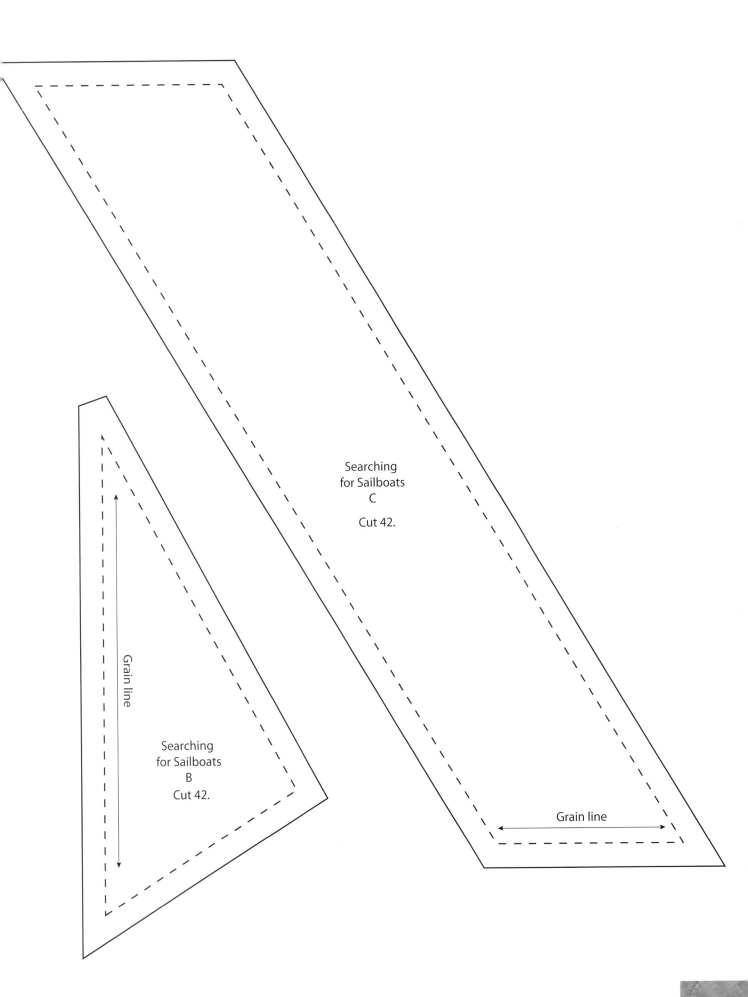

Searching
for Sailboats
C
Cut 42.

Grain line

Searching
for Sailboats
B
Cut 42.

Grain line

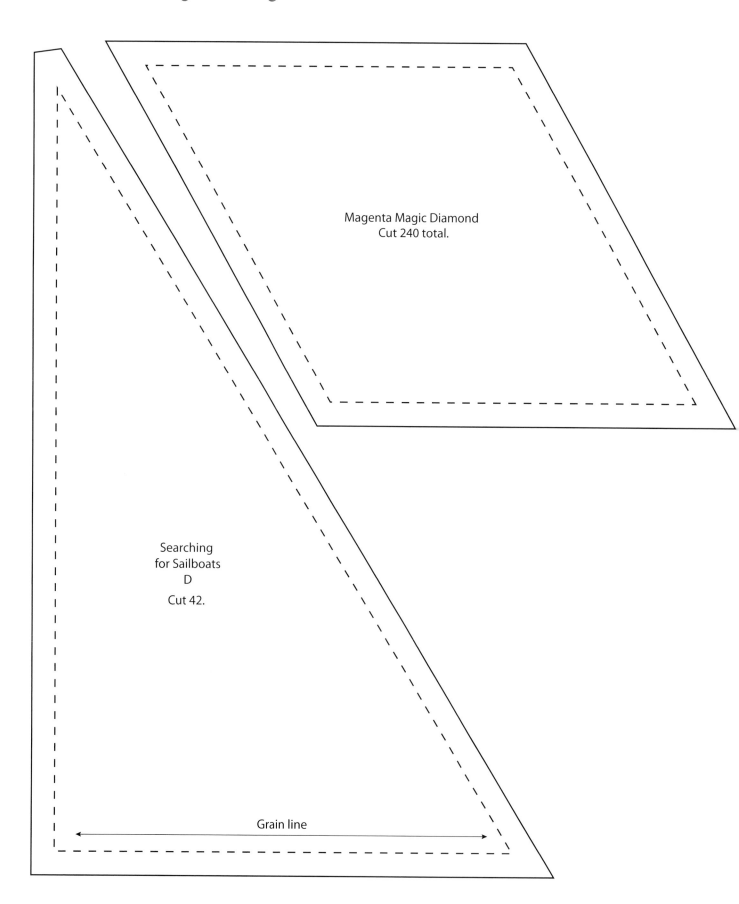

Magenta Magic Diamond
Cut 240 total.

Searching
for Sailboats
D
Cut 42.

Grain line

Seasons of Sunsets

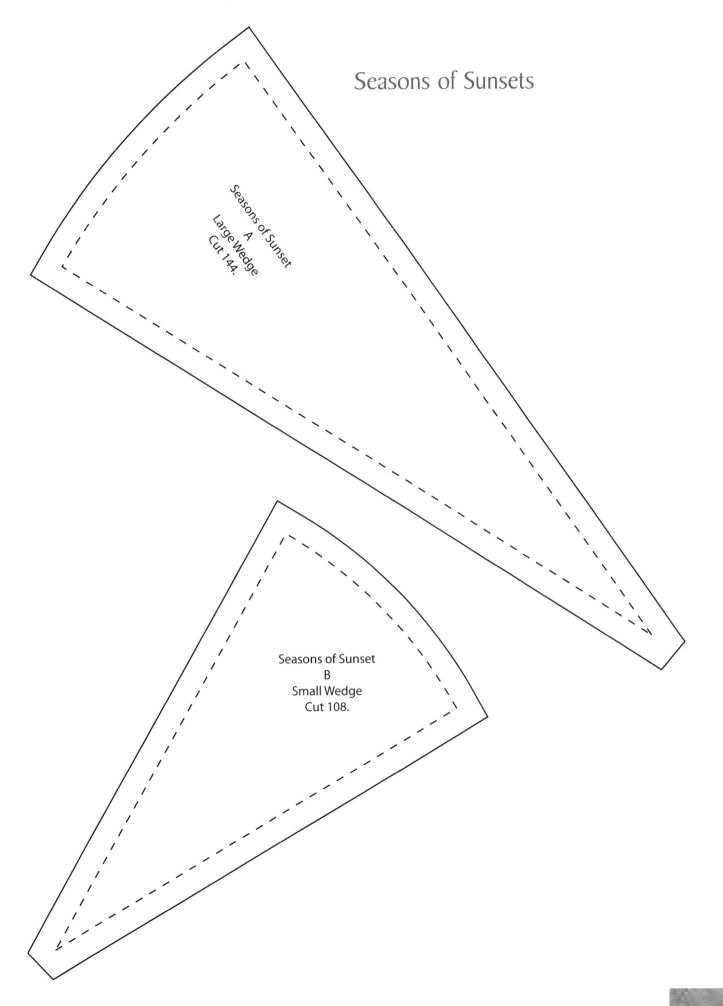

Seasons of Sunset
A
Large Wedge
Cut 144.

Seasons of Sunset
B
Small Wedge
Cut 108.

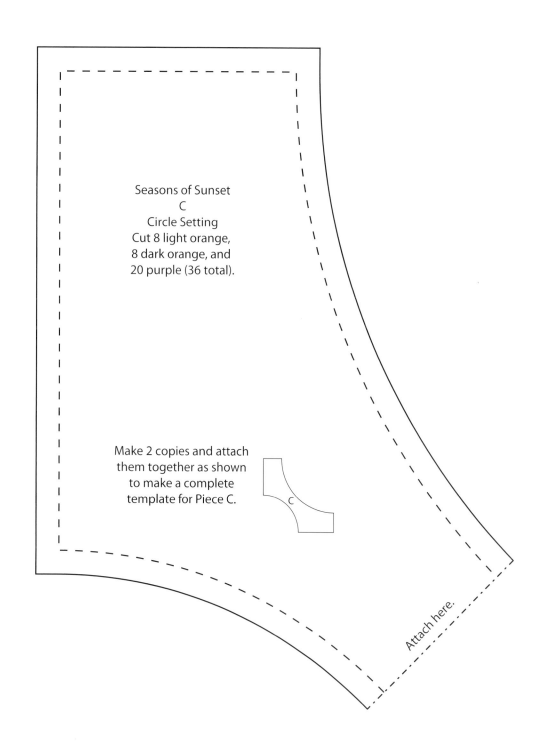

Seasons of Sunset
C
Circle Setting
Cut 8 light orange,
8 dark orange, and
20 purple (36 total).

Make 2 copies and attach
them together as shown
to make a complete
template for Piece C.

C

Attach here.

From Spain with Love

Resources

For fabrics:

Just for Fun Fabrics
2801 Old Greenwood Road,
Suite 12
Fort Smith, AR 72903
www.Jfffabrics.com
www.RobertaCardew.com
www.Cardew-Spain.com

About the Author

Roberta Cardew

Although relatively new to quilting, Roberta is certainly no stranger to the needle arts, having been born into a sewing-oriented family. She grew up in a small town in Ohio, her young life crowded with music lessons, baking cookies, growing flowers, and sewing her way through summers of 4-H projects. She attended Mills College near San Francisco to study math, and after college followed her heart to Paris to pursue a longtime committment to music. In Paris, she continued her study of the piano at the Conservatory and made a brave attempt to master the French language, attending classes at the University of Paris. Throughout all these years, the common thread was sewing: for herself, for friends, for free, for pay, for the joy of it. She was never without a sewing machine!

Roberta is married to an eminent English studio potter and sculptor, Seth Cardew, and they divide their time between their home in Spain and the United States, where Roberta owns and operates a fabric/quilt shop, Just for Fun Fabrics.

Roberta's three children are grown, and her one grandchild is in college.

In addition to quilting and fabric bolts enough to fill a shop, her basic requirements are flower gardens, good compost, a small orchard, a kitchen that is big enough, and an excellent and well-tuned piano—and, of course, pleasant people and plenty of patchwork.

Molly Ware

Molly Ware, the photographer for *From Spain with Love*, is Roberta's youngest child. She attended secondary school in England and studied history and liberal arts at the University of Arkansas. Her interests lie in the artistic domain and especially include photography. She presently resides in Edinburgh, Scotland.

Great Titles *from* C&T PUBLISHING

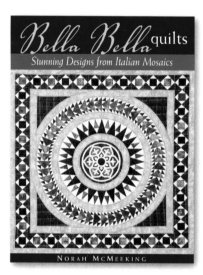

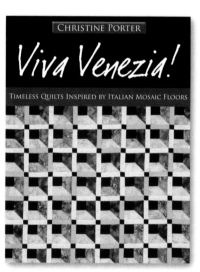

Available at your local retailer or **www.ctpub.com** *or* **800-284-1114**

For a list of other fine books from C&T Publishing, ask for a free catalog:

C&T PUBLISHING, INC.
P.O. Box 1456
Lafayette, CA 94549
800-284-1114

Email: ctinfo@ctpub.com
Website: www.ctpub.com

C&T Publishing's professional photography services are now available to the public. Visit us at www.ctmediaservices.com.

Tips and Techniques can be found at www.ctpub.com > Consumer Resources > Quiltmaking Basics: Tips & Techniques for Quiltmaking & More

For quilting supplies:

COTTON PATCH
1025 Brown Ave.
Lafayette, CA 94549
Store: 925-284-1177
Mail order: 925-283-7883

Email: CottonPa@aol.com
Website: www.quiltusa.com

Note: Fabrics used in the quilts shown may not be currently available, as fabric manufacturers keep most fabrics in print for only a short time.